Joseph A. H.

THE
HAINT

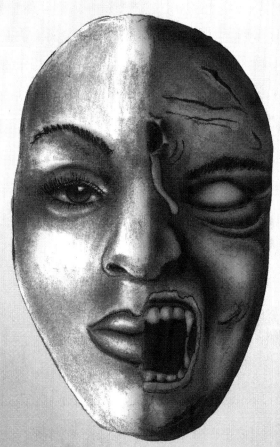

illustrated by
Christopher Evans

Joseph A. Eddington's

THE
HAINT

• • •

This book is dedicated to my mother Bernice Eddington to whom I owe my existence to. She is the person who introduced me to God, until that introduction she was my God. She stayed in my life, making sure I never fell short of being the best I could be. She still runs her finger under my shirt making sure I am wearing a T Shirt. She gave Ashanti her virtues and goodness as well as some of her ferocity. My book is filled with many of her sayings. I love you mommy and this book is dedicated to you. Peace and Love

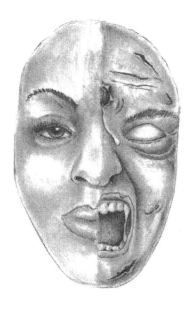

I would like to thank Charlie Barrios my a alike mind, Lisa Thomson Howard my friend and confidant, Tanea Eddington my first born daughter, Dr.Garner who always had the time and Mr. Aleem who was my high school teacher and the most influential teacher in my life. These Individuals played a major part in supporting me in various endevors of my book.

In Memory Of Mario Flintroy, Micheal Puzzo, Greg Lee, Robert Smith AKA Stinker and all others who have passed on rest in Peace. Also thanks to Ms. Garrett, because without her, I would have never discovered my talent.

• • •

—————— Prologue ——————

It is the beginning of the morning, and the rim of the sun is coming up over the horizon at the start of another African day. An old man is walking down a path that he has walked many times before. The morning dew has made the bottom of his robe wet. As he passes by a Baobab tree he hears screaming. The old man looks to the left, then to the right before pin pointing where the screams are coming from. They are coming from a thick patch of grass just ahead of him. As he draws closer the crying gets louder. When he reaches the source of the crying he cautiously bends down and parts the tall grass with his hands. To his amazement, the old man discovers a baby bundled up lying in the grass. As the baby looks up at him it begins to smile, exposing its deeply pronounced dimples, just as if it already knew that the old man is its savior.

The old man's heart fills with joy as he picks the child up. The child begins cooing and continues smiling at the old man. The old man's expression changes as he puts the baby back into the tall grass. By keeping this child he knows that it would violate a taboo. The child was put there because it has violated some village law. The old man turns around and begins walking down the path and tries to ignore the screaming child. As he takes a few more steps he hears the child scream out something that sounded like: "Moooojoooo!" The image of the child appears in his mind, so he quickly turns around and picks the child up again and heads towards the opposite way up the path. The old man is going back to his hut which is on the outskirts of the village whose inhabitants he heals and rids of evil spirits. He is the village witch doctor. He is called "Mojo, the Medicine Man".

He has grey hair that curls down toward a bald spot in the middle of his head which makes it look like he is wearing a crown. He has three long broad wrinkles just above his eyebrows that stretch across his forehead which make him look serious even when he is joking. He always walks with a wooden staff that has animals carved in it. Even though he is elderly, his words are strong and stern when he speaks. His legs look as though they are carved out of the same wood his staff is made of. One of his eyes has no color in the center of it, and if you look at it long enough, it will put you in a trance. Mojo is always serious, rarely ever smiling.

When a child is left out to die, it is because the child's existence has broken one of the taboos in a village. It could be a strange birth mark on the child's body or a tragedy that happened just before or after the child is born. Like a mass sickness in the village or an attack by an enemy tribe that caused a lot of death and destruction to the village. Violators of such taboos have been banned from the village for life and some have even been stoned to death.

When Mojo arrives back at his hut he commands his assistant, "Go to the village and get some goat's milk". His assistant asks, "why?" The doctor opens up the cloth and lays the baby on a mat. His assistant knows what Mojo has done and shakes his head as he skittishly backs away. Mojo yells, "Mansa, get over here! This child called out my name, she is the chosen one". Mojo tells Mansa that the child called his name out in order to persuade him.

Mansa is Mojo's assistant; he is in his mid - twenties. He is a tall, wiry, dark brown skinned young man. He always has a sneaky look on his face, as if he is going to create mischief.

"Mojo, I don't want nothing to do with that child, I don't want any harm to come to me", exclaims Mansa.

"Mansa, just go to the village and get some goat milk," replies Mojo.

Mansa looks at Mojo with a perplexed look, scratching his head and says, "For you Mojo, I will do it."

Mansa begins to walk down the path heading toward the village. Mojo rocks the baby as they smile at each other. Mojo realizes that the baby is a girl after he unwraps the cloth that swaddles her and he bathes her. After bathing her, he wraps her in a new Kente cloth.

When Mansa arrives he has a bowl of goat's milk and an animal lining that will be used as a bottle and a nipple. Mansa tells Mojo, "She must be special for you to wrap her in the cloth that you were going to have your ceremonial robe made from". Mojo looks down at her and replies, "Yes, she is special".

"Mojo, what will you tell the villagers?"

"I will tell them that my sister is sick and I will raise her daughter. My sister lives in a village many days travel from here. They will never see her to ask her anything," he continues.

"I will raise this child myself."

"And I will help you."

"What will you call her Mojo?"

"I will call her Ashanti."

Chapter I

As an infant, Ashanti is very curious about her surroundings. She crawls around grabbing and pulling things down. Every day, while Mojo prepares his medicine she sits watching his every move as if she is studying him. One day while she is watching him, he purposely puts the wrong ingredient into one of his mixtures. She looks at him as if she knows what has just happened, which makes Mojo laugh out loud, which also startles Mansa because he knows that Mojo doesn't laugh very often. Mansa steps out of the hut,

"Mojo, what tickled you so?"

"Ashanti."

"What about her?"

"While I work my medicine, she always watches me, as if she knows what I am doing. So I purposely put the wrong ingredients in this bowl and she looked at me as if to say, That's not right."

Mansa begins to laugh as well, at what Mojo has just told him.

They both take turns watching Ashanti while waiting for the right time to take her to the village. Ashanti begins walking and talking at an early age. She calls Mojo, "Momo" and Mansa "Mana." Now, when she watches Mojo she always says "what dat Momo, what dat?", and he always tells her what it is. She learns how to walk before she turns one and starts talking well before she turns two. One day, when Mojo thinks she is old enough, he fixes a harness made out of cloth and carries her gently, hanging from his back heading to the village.

On their way they start playing a game.

"What dat Momo?"

"A grass hopper"

"What dat Momo?"

"A bird"

"What dat?"

"You know what that is. What's that Ashanti?" as he points at a cloud.

"A dowd"

"What is that?"

"A doat"

They continue to play this game until they arrive at their village, which is named Kisumu.

When they arrive, the whole village comes out to greet them, as if the village already knew they were coming. Mojo takes Ashanti off his back and holds her in his arms. Ashanti's eyes open wide since she has never seen so many people before in her life. As they get closer to the people, Ashanti reaches out and touches whoever comes close to her, as if she is making herself familiar with everyone. She is not shy at all, the people love her and she loves her people as well. The chief asks Mojo, "Since when do you have a baby?" Snickering as he speaks. Mojo does not like to lie, "She is a gift from the heavens," he replies. Mojo doesn't have to say anything else; the village immediately accepts Ashanti.

Time goes by quickly and Ashante turns ten. Even though she is mature for her age she is still watched by the villagers while Mojo and Mansa take care of business there. Mansa isn't always able to come and help Mojo but they both don't have to worry about taking care of Ashanti since the villagers always offer to take care of and watch her. They even sometimes argue over the right to take care of her. They bathe her, dress her and even ornamentally braid her hair. The entire village helps Mojo raise Ashanti.

One evening as they are getting ready to leave, one of the villagers who watched Ashanti for the whole day, comes to Mojo so he can relieve her of her duties.

"How was she?"

"She was fine" says the villager as she tickles Ashanti to make her show off her pretty dimples.

"Thank you, and what do you want for your services?" The lady looks at him as if he has said something wrong, "Now, Mojo, you know better than to offer me payment with all that you have done for my family but if you insist may I offer you a suggestion?

"What's that?"

"Get her a little puppy because she loves animals. She tries to call every animal she sees so she can pet them. For some reason, they all seem to come to her".

Mojo nods to the lady, then wraps Ashanti in her cloth and puts her on his back and starts heading back to his hut. They are also joined by Mansa, who meets them at the beginning of the path.

One evening, during dinner, a wild cat comes close to their hut following the smell of food. Ashanti tries to run up to it but as soon as she gets too close the cat disappears in the bushes.

On another evening, while they are sitting by their pot over the fire, the same wild cat drops a dead rat at the feet of Ashanti. The light of the fire illuminates the scene of the event that just took place. Mojo and Mansa understand the true meaning of what has just took place in their presence. Ashanti does not jump or is startled at all. She just takes a piece of meat out of her mouth and feeds it to the cat. After that evening the cat and Ashanti become good friends.

Mojo watches how the cat seems to be teaching Ashanti it's ways. Ashanti stands and the cat weaves through her legs, rubbing up and down arching it's back. Her tail wraps around her leg like a serpent as she passes. Ashanti stretches her back and arches like the cat as well. Playing with the cat Ashanti finds out that the cat is a female and names her Sheba. Ashanti follows Sheba as she stalks animals in the bush. In a strange way Ashanti develops the ability to be as quiet as Sheba as they both stalk pray. It is as if Sheba is teaching Ashanti the ways of a cat. Ashanti also notices how Sheba eases and arches her back and then sprays the bushes and trees around the hut. Ashanti wonders why the cat keeps doing this.

One morning, before the cat's arrival, Mojo is preparing his bag for the day. Ashanti steps out of the hut with some trinkets for Mojo to put in his bag. "Mojo, why does Sheba always spray around the bush?" "That's her way to let other animals know that this is her domain." Ashanti nods her head in acknowledgement of Mojo's reply.

The next evening Sheba sprays and meows very loudly. She will not come and give Ashanti any attention. It is as if Sheba is on a mission. That evening, after they finish having dinner, and while they are sitting around with full bellies, Ashanti looks at Mojo and says, "Mojo, Sheba only comes and sprays and won't let me touch her?"

"Sheba is ready to have a family, so she is singing in hopes that a male hears her and she sprays hoping that a male smells her, so she can mate with him."

Ashanti looks at Mojo with a look of perplexity on her face, not being able to understand what he just said. He smiles and rubs her head while saying, "I will tell you one day what the relationship between a man who loves a woman and wants to settle down and have a family is all about. Right now, you don't need to worry your pretty little head about such things."

Early next morning Ashanti hears loud screeches in the distance. She gets up and sneaks out and goes to the side of the hut and watches Sheba as she screams out to let the male cats that are making the noises from a far, know where she is. Ashanti hears screams coming from different directions as Sheba meows out loudly in their direction in order to get their attention. One of the cats walks out of the bushes and eases cautiously toward Sheba. As the cat approaches, Sheba arches her back and hisses at the coming suitor, turning her back at him as she sprays him. The cat opens his mouth wide, reacting from the aroma from her spray.

Sheba walks up to the cat, rubbing herself across him, as if she is drying herself off on him.

Two other cats come out of the bushes as well and walk up to Sheba as she hisses at them in the same fashion as she did the first cat. The three cats start fighting making noises that would wake up even the devil. The scene awakens Mojo and Mansa, who walk toward where the fighting is going on. As the three cats fight, Sheba walks away in a very sexy manner and disappears into the bushes looking over her shoulder, making sure that her suitors notice her leaving. The cats suddenly stop fighting and start running after Sheba disappearing into the bushes.

Mojo looks at Ashanti to see what her reaction is. Ashanti looks like she has just learned about the power of a female. Ashanti, just like her feline friend, rises out of her crouch and gracefully sways back and forth toward the front of their hut after witnessing the spectacle. Mojo and Mansa look at each other as if they were ready to say, "No, she didn't." They have just witnessed Ashanti's personification of Sheba. Ashanti continues to move in ways that are too provocative for someone her age. Mojo and Mansa will promptly correct her every time she behaves this way around them.

Time goes by and Ashanti does not see Sheba for a couple months. One morning she hears tiny meows and she springs forth and runs outside in her night dress. Sheba is in the back of the hut with four little kittens following behind her. Ashanti stops in her tracks, knowing that she can no longer approach Sheba. Sheba looks at Ashanti as if to say, "This is my family, you are now on your own." A sad feeling fills Ashanti's heart as Sheba leads her new family back into the bushes while looking over her shoulder at Ashanti for the last time. Ashanti's heart is also filled with glee from now knowing that she has new brothers and sisters.

Time continues to pass and Ashanti has become a young lady. She has a shiny cocoa colored complexion which accents her dimples when she smiles. Her teeth are white and she has the body of a young woman with the face of a thirteen year old girl. Her lips are full, which accents her dimples even more. Her hair is ornately braided with cowry shells. She also wears a necklace made of cowry beads mixed with pretty stones in between each shell; a cloth pouch hangs at the end of the necklace with a pretty stone in the center of it. The pouch is filled with herbs and other concoctions that Mojo has taught her about. She always wears a pretty gown made of soft linen that makes her look like a young princess. The girls in the village have always braided Ashanti's hair ever since she was a young child. She has been raised by the village's witch doctor who has taught her everything he knows. For years Mojo takes Ashanti to the outskirts of the village in order to study nature. He does this in order to teach her how significant nature is to their lives.

Overtime, Mojo discovers that Ashanti has a gift of attracting all kinds of animals. Stray antelope fawns often come and eat right out of her hand. Mojo has to scold her over and over again because other animals that hunt them could start being too close to their home. It seems as if she can talk to birds, and livestock follow her whenever she goes into the village. She tries to learn as much as she can from anything and everything. From watching Mojo as he prepares his concoctions, to watching how the villagers rotate their crops.

Mojo also teaches Ashanti all about the Gods and where each one of them stands in his life. While teaching, Mojo tells her, "Ashanti, Obatalá is the God of all creation. When Obatalá does his handy work, he molds people out of clay and then Olotumari breathes life into them. There are also many lesser Gods, and Shango is my favorite. He is the God of lightning and war. Shango lights up the sky in the same manner I light up the hearts and souls of my people with my medicinal healing."

"Ashanti, this is very important, what I'm about to say"

"Everything you say is important to me, Mojo"

"Yes, yes, dear, I know, but I want you to pay close attention to what I'm about to tell you," as he softly pinches her on her cheek near her dimple.

"Gaunab is the God of evil and wickedness. Never mess with him in any kind of way, because if you do, he will bring destruction and death your way. Even though he is evil, he is responsible for the creation of rainbows. Don't let that fool you, he is evil, make sure that you never forget." Ashanti nods yes.

Mojo smiles as Ashanti listens to him as if his words create life. He will often remind her, "Never use what I have taught you for evil. Use it only for good purposes. Bad things will happen to you if you work it for negativity. Also, don't forget, mother earth is alive, always be at one with her. By doing so, you will always be constant with the universe. Remember earth is our mother".

While saying this he picks up some soil and pours it into her hand as if he is losing sand out of an hour glass. Mojo points his index finger toward Ashanti and uses it to lift her face by the chin. He looks into her eyes, "Never forget this, my dear, there is nothing greater than you in this universe; you understand me?" Ashanti nods her head yes and leans over and hugs Mojo as hard as she can. Mojo has also taught Ashanti the enchantments of magic. She recites them over and over while she is doing her daily chores. One of Mojo's favorite words when he ends his incantations is Zooka Mallie.

One of the things that Mojo enjoys the most is Ashanti's cooking which he boasts to everyone about how good it tates. He also notices the way in which Ashanti reacts every time she sees a rainbow. She jumps around in excitement, looking up at nature's color menagerie. She always goes into the same state of excitement every time she sees one. It is almost as if she has never seen one before. This reaction to rainbows on the part of Ashanti actually puzzles Mojo. He shakes and scratches his head in bewilderment as she goes into this frenzy.

Mojo does not really understand the significance of her actions.

Chapter II

Ashanti is becoming a medicine woman. In fact, she has already surpassed the knowledge of Mojo's assistant, Mansa. Over time, Mansa starts becoming jealous of Ashanti. He notices that the villagers will ask her for help before asking him. Every time Ashanti enters the village the village's Griot announces her as royalty. The Griot is the person who greets visitors and royalty when they come to the village. They usually have a very strong voice and are aware of all the events in and around the village.

"Ladies and gentlemen, Ashanti the medicine woman has arrived to our village of Kisumu!"

Ashanti smiles, showing her dimples, as she waves to the villagers and they wave back at her, as she passes by. As she goes by, young children stop playing Kala just to greet her as well. She gets thrilled by this spectacle every time, as if it would be happening for the first time. One day, Mansa, after witnessing this, tries to make a grand entrance himself but he doesn't get the same reaction from the villagers. Only the elders of the village greet him, as they just sit under a tree waiting for his arrival to drink home brew.

Ashanti loves when the Griot tells stories about Anansi the spider. Mojo has told her some of the same stories as well. It is more fun when she is sitting around people her age when the Griot is telling stories about Anansi the spider.

One particular day, in a fatherly way, Mojo is admiring how beautiful Ashanti has become, as she is walking through the village. He stands near by as she is helping an elderly woman get to her hut. Ashanti drops a bowl by accident and immediately four young men run up to her to assist her. Ashanti smiles at them all, thanking them for trying to help her. She exudes her essence in the same way Sheba exudes her pheromones to attract a mate.

9

As she continues to walk with the elderly lady, the four young men stand and watch her, ripening womanhood in their minds. They seem as if they are in a semi conference, aroused by her beauty, while ripping her clothes off with their eyes. As they confer among themselves, one of them looks up and sees Mojo. The young man gets caught by Mojo's non colored eye. The other fellows wonder what made their buddy stop in his tracks. They all look up at the same time and witness it for themselves. They all quickly scurry like jackals running away from a lion's kill. Mojo has seen "The cat" being sassy and sexy, witnessing the effect she has on men. Mojo knows that the day will come when he will have to talk to Ashanti about when and how she will become a woman. He just doesn't know when and how he will do so. He turns around scratching his head with a perplexed look on his face.

Mojo has business to take care of in the village. That is the reason why he has hung around waiting to catch up with Ashanti. The village is going to have a celebration for the son of the chief who is getting married to a woman from a neighboring village. Since the groom is from Mojo's village, the wedding has to be hosted here. Mojo has to bless the bride and the groom as he has done ever since he became a medicine man.

After Ashanti finishes helping the old lady to her hut, she runs up to Mojo excited for the celebration that will be taking place in their village. "Mojo, I am ready to assist you with the wedding."

"Yeah, I know you are also ready to eat, sneak some of that home brew and then dance the night away."

"Yes, yes, Mojo I'm ready!"

As she is speaking she is twirling and jumping around as if she is practicing for the dance of the night. Ever since Ashanti was a little girl she has always enjoyed weddings and any celebration that takes place in the village.

Mansa, who has already started drinking the home brew, staggers over to Mojo and Ashanti, and begins to talk to Mojo with a slur, "Mojo, I will be ready to assist you during the wedding. Give me a nod and I will be right there." Mansa has assisted Mojo with many weddings over the years. Ever since Ashanti has gotten older Mansa's assistance has waned. Mojo looks at Mansa with a stern look, "Mansa, you go back over there and assist the elders with their home brew." Did you at least bring your tools and herbs so I can conduct the wedding?" Mansa shamefully bows his head and shakes it as to signify no.

Mojo stands in front of Mansa shaking his head in disgust, "Ashanti and I will take care of the wedding".

"I've got the right mind to make you go back home and get the ceremonial instruments for the wedding."

As Mojo is talking to Mansa Ashanti runs to a hut and takes a netted bag out of it and happily skips it to Mojo. Mojo and Mansa look into the bag at the same time. Mojo looks at Ashanti with a smile, pulling her toward him while giving her a big hug. Ashanti brought the material for the wedding along with the herbs needed. Mojo's expression quickly changes when he looks at Mansa. He turns around and walks the other way from Mansa with his arm around Ashanti.

As they get closer to the chief's home they can smell the wonderful scent of meat cooking. They walk to a large enclosure which is comprised of a large brownish wall. As they walk inside, the many wives of the chief greet them. To their left, there are people turning five butchered bulls over an open fire. They continue walking toward a very large hut inside the enclosure. When they reach the door, the chief Musa, steps out, as if he knew that they were coming. He is a large pot Bellied man with a goatee which he strokes when he is speaking. He has a leopard skin that wraps across his chest and Kente cloth surrounds his hip to his knees. He has thick legs that lead down to his sandaled feet. Ashanti and Mojo bow in unison to their chief. The chief hugs Mojo, then Ashanti. He shakes his head at Mojo, stretching and yawning before speaking.

"Mojo, I was up for most of the night at my son's bride's to be village negotiating her dowry so my son can marry her. We finally came up with a number of cattle that I had to give up so that the wedding can take place."

"You better start marrying off your daughters and start having more girls so your herd doesn't get depleted; by having daughters you would receive a dowry instead of having to give one." advised Mojo to the chief.

Musa pulls Mojo close to his ear and whispers to him, "Maybe you may have to work your magic on my baby maker so I can have only girls."

The people around them do not know what the chief had just whispered into Mojo's ear but they know that whatever it was, it made them both laugh.

As they speak, they begin to hear noise coming from the distance. Mojo leaves the compound to go get Musa's son. The noise keeps coming closer as Mojo returns with the groom who is surrounded by men from the other village. From around a grove of trees comes a large group of villagers from the neighboring village of the bride. The women are wailing and their men are just walking beside them. The drums start banging out loud announcing the coming of the bride. In the middle of the crowd walks the bride surrounded by women of her village. They all merge at the entrance of the gate, proceeding in until they are all inside the compound.

The chief's son stands between the chief and Mojo. The crowd keeps drawing closer and closer until finally it comes to a complete stop. Suddenly, the crowd opens up like the mouth of a hippo. A small crowd of women comes forward stopping just before, Mojo the groom and the chief. The crowd of related women directly opens slowly and gracefully exposing the beautiful bride. She slowly walks toward Mojo, the chief and the groom. The chief steps back and sits on his throne, surrounded by his many wives and children. The bride is wearing golden Kente clothe which wraps around her head and lower torso. Both arms are full of gold bracelets that can be heard clinging every time she moves her arms. The groom has a leopard skin that drapes across his chest and Kente cloth covering his lower torso. He is a smaller version of his father. Mojo looks at Ashanti and she hands him a silk piece of cloth, which he ties around the arm of the bride and groom, binding them together as one.

Mojo puts one hand on top each of their heads. He recites, "May all the Gods bless you, keeping you together forever. May you have many beautiful and healthy children. May your cattle be many and your harvest vast". Mojo then pushes their heads downward, guiding them to their knees. Ashanti hands him an ox tail that is bounded with leather from bottom to top and at the very end, the hair of the ox flows outward and drapes all around the leather. Mojo shakes the ox tail over the heads of the newlyweds as he chants. He hands the tail back to Ashanti and she pours white grounded roots, which they use for healing, in the palm of Mojo's hand.

Mojo continues to chant before blowing the white powder over their faces and heads. He has them stand up, turning them towards the crowd, and says, "Under the Heavens, they are now one with the Universe." The crowd yells out in respect and celebration of the newly wedded couple. The newlyweds are then escorted to an open tent where they get congratulated and gifts are laid at their feet.

The music starts playing and people start bouncing to its rhythm. Ashanti can feel the rhythm flowing through her entire body. The five slaughtered bulls continue to be turned over the open fires that are slowly making the meat ready for consumption. The smell is so good that Ashanti can almost taste the food without having eaten it. Everyone begins to drink and be merry. Then they begin to dance as the music seems to get louder and louder and more and more intense with each beating of the drums.

One of the young men hands Ashanti a cup of home brew and she starts sipping on it. Mojo walks by, "All right, now I see you; you better take it easy." Ashanti smiles as Mojo walks by her. Ashanti starts dancing, allowing the music to take over her body. Her cat- like movements get the young and old men excited as they watch her moving as they become mesmerized. The dancing and celebration goes on into the night. Ashanti dances and sips on her brew as the night continues on.

Ashanti sees Mojo talking with some of the village's elders with his head slightly bent downward. As she gets closer to them she can hear his words slurring as they come out of his mouth. She points her finger at him.

"All right, all right, you better take it easy with that brew!" exclaims Ashanti. They both laugh as they take another sip and give each other another toast.

The celebration is over and Mojo, Ashanti and Mansa walk down the path that leads them to their home. Ashanti does her best to hold the two older men as they walk going side to side as much as they move forward. They get home and they all lay down for the night.

Chapter III

Next morning Ashanti rushes out of the hut screaming. Mansa and Mojo are already outside getting ready for the day. They are still hung over from the previous night as they sluggishly look over some herbs and other healing remedies that they will need for the day. Ashanti runs past them and Mojo sees blood on one of her hands. He motions to Mansa for him to go to the village and get one of the sisters to help with this issue. Mojo grabs a cloth, puts it in water and then wrings it out. He follows the drips of blood and calls Ashanti's name. She is reluctant to answer, but does so anyways.

"Yes Mojo, I'm here," she is squatting behind a tree waiting for him. Mojo turns his back toward where he hears the voice coming from. He then walks backwards facing the opposite direction handing her the wet cloth. He tells Ashanti, "This is the sign of you becoming a woman. Because this has happened, you are now able to have a child. So let no man touch you or lay down with you because the result could be the birth of a child. Someone will be here to talk to you and assist you," Mojo turns around and sees Ashanti with her head down. He reaches down with his finger and lifts her head by her chin and smiles at her. Not long after a woman from the village comes to assist Ashanti with her womanhood.

Mojo continues to witness how Ashanti exudes her essence as she walks through the village. One day after the harvest, some young men gather by a granary drinking home brew. Ashanti weaves through the men with the grace of a cheetah, slowly stalking, just before making its mad dash to run its victim down, without touching the men. As she passes by, each man's posture changes, as if they have become immersed in Ashanti's essence. Young and older men approach her; she never gives them the time of the day in that way. As she reaches Mojo, he puts his arm around her and says, "Listen Ashanti, you must control that."

"Control what, Mojo?"

"You know what I'm talking about. The seductive ways you have learned from Sheba, attracting mates."

Ashanti smiles, exposing her dimples, and turns away not to let Mojo know that she is laughing at what she knows to be true.

"But Mojo, I don't touch males or look at them in that way."

"I know Ashanti, but you are getting the reputation of being a tease, which makes men angry. Women are starting to talk about it as well. You don't want any rumors to be spread. Just turn your spray off, ok?"

While Mojo is saying this he puts his arm around her neck letting it drape over her shoulder while in the other hand he is holding a bag which is draped over his back. Ashanti looks up at him and says, "Ok Mojo," as she holds his walking stick and she herself becomes sort of a human walking stick for him as Mojo leans on her. Ashanti tipping with Mojo's cane, walks down the path that leads them back to their hut as the big orange African sun sets over the horizon.

Years go by and Ashanti is still blooming and blossoming. She has stopped exuding Sheba's ways in which she used to attract the bees to the flower, but would give no nectar. She cannot help herself when she dances at the village's celebrations, which gets the attention of all men who surround and watch her.

One afternoon Mojo, Ashanti and Mansa are at the hut getting ready for the next day. Their hut appears to be small when looked at from the outside, but it is in fact huge inside. It seems as though it is an optical illusion. Mojo has a room that is partitioned by long baby tree trunks. Mansa sleeps in the main room, which houses the ceremonial altar. On it seat leather pouches full of roots and herbs that he uses for healing and ceremonies. Ashanti sleeps in a room behind the altar.

Mojo calls out, "Mansa, make me a potion for bad fever." Mansa immediately jumps up off his mat, runs to the altar and starts mixing herbs in a gourd. As he is doing so, Ashanti tries to help him out. Mansa snarls at Ashanti saying, "I don't need your help; I was mixing this before you were even born." He brings the gourd to Mojo, who in turn sniffs it and pours some of its content on the palm of his hand. Mojo throws it on the ground and yells out,

"Mansa, you should be studying and practicing your craft instead of drinking beer with the village elders all day. Be gone with you!" As Mansa is leaving he notices that Ashanti has prepared her own concoction. Mansa looks back to see how Mojo reacts to the concoction Ashanti brings to him. Mojo smells it, then pours some of it on the palm of his hand and smiles as he says, "Maybe you will be my heir when I leave this earth." Mansa put his head down in a cowering manner and bends down in order to leave the hut.

The next day Mansa over hears a conversation between Mojo and Ashanti. Mojo yells out, "Ashanti, come here!" Ashanti puts some bones and other object back into a bowl before coming to Mojo.

"Yes Mojo."

"I am hearing a lot of good things about you from the villagers. You know that I am getting old and I don't know how much longer I will be on this earth. You will have to take over for me."

"But what about Mansa?"

"He is not as good as you; he hasn't taken these studies seriously," answers Mojo with a reassuring look on his face.

"Mojo, I am also a woman. I have never seen or heard of a woman witch doctor before!" she yells out with her hands on her hips.

"The villagers don't even notice. They still always come for your help. Don't worry Ashanti, you will be just fine".

Mansa has a very discouraged look on his face after over hearing Mojo and Ashanti's conversation. The expression on his face begins to change as he starts to develop a sinister plan to get rid of Ashanti. He starts to smile with a menacing look on his face, just like a hyena that is getting ready to steal a meal, as he rubs his hands together. Mansa has heard of slave traders making raids in nearby villages. He will send Ashanti on a mission to one of these villages, hoping that she gets captured.

Next morning Mansa meets Ashanti at the river while she is washing their clothes.

"Ashanti, Mojo wants you to go to the nearest village to get some roots that he will need for our ceremony tonight".

"Mojo never mentioned anything to me about picking anything up from another village."

"He forgot, so he sent me down here to let you know." Go ahead Ashanti;

I will finish washing the clothes for you."

Ashanti leaves for the nearest village to get the roots for the ceremony, without knowing that she is leaving never to return again. She is later that day captured by white slave traders. As she is being brought in chains along with others who have just been captured, she looks at a crowd of people and sees Mansa and calls his name. He turns around to see who is calling, when he realizes that it is Ashanti he bows his head in disgrace. As Mansa shamefully shrugs his shoulders he is led away, also bound in chains.

Ashanti has been caught by slave traders and is on her way to get shipped to America where she will be sold into a life of bondage.

Chapter IV

Days have gone by and Mojo hasn't heard anything from Mansa or Ashanti. He has walked the path many times into the village trying to find out if anybody has seen or heard anything, but to no avail. One morning he hears a knock on his hut's door. He jumps up as fast as an old man can. He opens the door, still rubbing his eyes, hoping it is Mansa or Ashanti. When he opens the door there is a young man on one knee. He asks the young man to stand on his feet. The young man rises slowly and majestically before he starts speaking in a very low tone of voice. Mojo yells out "Speak up, young man!"

"Mojo, my chief and the elders sent me here to give you this message".

"Speak on!"

"We have not had a good crop in years and we need your help."

"What about Hoodoo?" inquires Mojo? Hoodoo is their village's witch doctor.

We have tried everything and our village has only gotten meager yields from our crops."

"Ok young man. I will be there tomorrow. You will have to make this journey with me because I am an old man".

The young man looks at Mojo and quickly turns his head away in respect. He has heard of the tales about looking into Mojo's colorless eye. Next day they travel to the young man's village. Upon their arrival the village's Griot announces them, "Ladies and gentlemen, Mojo has arrived at our village".

The chief and the elders usher Mojo under a tree where they all sit down to discuss this issue. The chief points toward the end of the village, where Hoodoo lives, in order to give the doctor a synopsis of what has been going on. After being directed where to go, Mojo starts walking toward the edge of the village where Hoodoo, their medicine man lives. Just as Mojo gets to

Hoodoo's hut, Hoodoo steps out. He is a little bit shorter than Mojo. He has a feather as an ornament piercing in his left ear. He has a dusty gray complexion, as if he bathes in ashes from a camp fire. The center of his head is bald with gray curled hair around it. It makes him look like he is wearing a crown. His fingers are sharply pointed as if he could poke a hole through you. His face has a few wrinkles for a man of his age, but the stress of the failure of the crops is visible all over his face. Hoodoo and Mojo embrace each other with respect and admiration.

"Mojo, I need you to help us." I have tried everything, but to no avail. Our crops continue to fail year after year. I know what is wrong and I have tried everything to bypass the problem. You have to fix this issue, Mojo."

Mojo looks at Hoodoo with a perplexed look on his face. "Me? How do I have anything to do with this?"

Hoodoo points to a hut that is not far from his which is on the out skirts of the village as well. Hoodoo hugs Mojo again and Mojo starts walking towards that particular hut. When Mojo arrives, he sees a man fixing his hut as his wife is cooking dinner in a black pot set on an open fire. The man stops what he is doing and walks over to Mojo and shakes his hand. Mojo says to the man, "What do you have to tell me?" The man's shoulders drop as he begins telling Mojo his story.

My wife and I were very young and recently married when we began trying to have a child. We tried for years and my wife could still not conceive a baby. We did everything Hoodoo advised us to do, but to no avail. We prayed to all the Gods as well but we still could not conceive. We finally were at our wits end when my wife came up with an idea. "Let's ask Gaunab to bless us with a child," said she. I immediately told my wife, "No, Gaunab is evil." My wife insisted in doing so, since she wanted to have a child so badly. I didn't want to, but she convinced me. We began to ask and worship Gaunab by doing animal sacrifices and praying to him every day. One morning I came out to tend to the fields and I saw a rainbow over our house. I called my wife and she was very happy to see the rainbow. As evil as Gaunab is, he is the God responsible for the creation of rainbows.

Our child was born at midnight, when the moon was full. It was a girl and my wife and I were really happy. The morning right after I walked outside to stretch, to my horror there was a hyena, a lion and a leopard sitting side by side, about twenty feet from our front door. I started hearing screaming coming toward me.

It was Hoodoo along with other villagers who were throwing rocks and making loud noises to run these beasts away. When they got closer the beasts ran off from the noises the villagers were making. Hoodoo ran up to me shouting, "What have you and your wife done?" *My wife steps out of our hut with our daughter in her arms and Hoodoo told her,* "You both know what has to be done with her." *My wife screamed out in horror and ran back into the hut.*

I reluctantly ran inside the hut and snatched my daughter from my wife's arms. I then started running with her away from the village. I ran a long way trying to rid my mind of what I knew I was about to do. I laid her among a bunch of tall grass, with my heart full of grief I took off running; remembering her pretty smile and her pronounced dimples as I ran. I ran away, hurting inside, as fast as I could. Every stride was harder to make because my legs began to weigh me down with grief."

Mojo asks, "How long ago was this?" The man's wife answers, "Our daughter would be turning eighteen within three full moons; on her next birthday." Mojo is shocked at what he has just heard and he thinks to himself, "What have I done?" He envisions Ashanti dancing around in delight after witnessing a rainbow in the sky. In slow motion, the vision of Ashanti dancing, skipping and whirling at the sight of a rainbow goes through his mind. Mojo doesn't know what he has unleashed by saving Ashanti. His muscles begin to tighten and the wrinkles on his forehead turn into ridges. His eyes widen and his colorless eye becomes like a beacon of powerful light that forces the man and woman to look away from his face. His muscles begin to loosen and his gaze becomes restrained. He then becomes subdued by the thought of him telling Ashanti to always use what he has taught her for good as they both stared into the evening's sky, into the universe.

Chapter V

Ashanti has marched for three days having had very little food or water. They feed her only a little bread and water each day. She gets her sustenance from the contents of her pouch by inhaling it. She has a chain around her neck that is attached to another woman. Her arms are tied tightly behind her back by a rope. She is both, angry and confused by the actions of these pale, bad smelling men. *One of them looks at me in a way that makes me feel very uncomfortable. I always avoid eye contact every time he looks at me. These men speak a language that I have never heard before. As each day passes by, I look at the faces of people who seem to be losing all hope; crying in tongues that I am familiar and unfamiliar with. The men are kept separate from the women by having them march in lines that are about forty feet away from each other. The white men hit and prod my people with sticks. Those who are not able to continue walking are left where they have fallen. The white men point sticks that spit fire and smoke at them. After a big bang, the body goes limp and starts spewing blood. These white men seem to be full of anger and hate. They don't seem to care about the blood they shed nor the lives they destroy.*

On the morning of the seventh day, they begin their journey again. Ashanti suspects that they are getting closer to their destination because the white men are edgy and are trying to make them move faster. At the end of the tree line Ashanti sees a lot of blue and white. All of a sudden the trees end and the sand begins. She looks out and sees an endless amount of blue water. Mojo has told her about the ocean before and of how the breeze tastes salty. *I see more villagers gathered about a half a mile away from where we came out of the forest. There are also more white men and more captives. I notice people who look like me seem to have had something to do with my people being captured since they have no chains on them and have fire sticks as well. Looking out into the ocean I can see very large canoes with white clothes that seem to catch the wind. As I look further down the beach I see a large hut made of stone. At the end of the hut there are very large canoes with large clothes that are folded down so they don't catch the wind. The white men continue to herd us toward the stone hut.*

As Ashanti walks through the entrance of the stone hut she is met by the terrible smell of death and despair. They are led into big smelly rooms with big hard doors. Ashanti's people are cramped into these rooms so tightly that they can barely breathe. What makes it worse is that through the night people die and drop onto the floor, making it very difficult for the others to even stand up straight.

The morning comes and the door is opened. The captives are led through a big hallway that has a light at the end of it. When Ashanti reaches the end of the tunnel the light blinds her and she can't see. She puts her head down until her eyes can bring the world back into focus. When her eyes clear and she can see again the first face she sees is the face of the white man that has been looking at her, making her feel uncomfortable throughout her entire journey.

He smiles at me, then looks at the large canoe and looks back at me and smiles again. The captives are loaded on the smaller canoes and then the white men start paddling toward the large canoes with the big wind catchers that have been dropped out of the air. My spirit is low because I don't know what I have gotten myself into. I don't know where this journey will end. When we got to the big canoe I notice a man with a beard standing on a level higher than the other white men. He seems to be telling everyone what to do. I guess he is the chief of this big canoe.

The white men ease the small canoe sideways next to the big canoe. Then everybody begins climbing up a net to get into the big canoe. When I got to the top of the net I climbed over a wall to board the large canoe. The white man that had been making me feel uncomfortable by looking at me motions for me to come to him. I look up at the chief and catch the twinkle in his eye as he motions for me to come up to where he is standing. The other white man is not pleased with this as he seems to want me for himself. I smile at him as he passes by, which seems to make him even more upset as his ears turn red.

Two men come to Asshanti to escort her to the captain. When Ashanti gets to the bottom step, she tries to resist but it is to no avail because she is too weak from the journey and the two men are too strong for her. She stands in front of the chief who has pretty green eyes. She can see her own reflection in his eyes. She has never seen eyes this color before. They are the same color as a bird that used to follow her to the village.

The chief was older than most of the men that he controlled but not as old as Mojo. He has the look of wisdom on his face. It is obvious that he was a handsome man in his younger days. His black beard with touches of gray gives him the look of a chief. The clothes that he is wearing are different from the clothes of any of the other men on the big canoe. They have more shiny things all over his chest."

He motions with his arm for Ashanti to come closer to him. She looks past him as she sees her people going into the belly of this wind catching beast. He leaves Ashanti alone as he starts directing everyone on the ship. When all her people get loaded into the ship's belly the big white cloth begins to catch the wind and they start moving. The chief begins turning a large wooden wheel and gestures for Ashanti to come to him.

Ashanti slowly walks towards him and he puts an arm around her neck while still controlling the wheel with the other hand. He starts touching Ashanti in places that make her feel uncomfortable. She knows what this man wants; Mojo has already told her about it when she bled for the first time. She knows that she has to do something about it because she doesn't want to give him what he wants. She gestures to him about eating, and she makes motion to convey that she will cook for him. He smiles and yells out in a strange language and promptly another man leads Ashanti to where the food is prepared.

Ashanti starts putting things together to prepare a meal. She starts chopping, stirring, and mixing ingredients in a big black pot. When the meal is done she pours some into a bowl. Ashanti then pours some of the contents in her pouch hanging from her neck into the bowl as well, as she recites one of her incantations. Then she is led back to his sleeping quarters where she finds the chief, already seated at the table, as if he has been anticipating the meal. Ashanti hands him the bowl with her head down, backing away humbly. He is sitting at his table inside the large cabin that is on top of the big ship. He grabs the spoon and digs right into the bowl. Just before he puts the spoon into his mouth he waves his hand at Ashanti, inviting her to come to him. He puts the spoon into her mouth and makes her eat first. Ashanti does, he smiles and then he starts eating. She sits at the corner of his hut waiting, worrying whether or not the "Mojo" that she put in this man's food will work. After he finishes eating he walks out of his hut and starts ordering people around.

It is already night time when he finally walks back into his sleeping quarters.

He takes his clothes off and lays on his mat and motions for me to come to him. I am sweating and very scared. I am not ready for what he wants to do. I climb on his mat which is above the floor and lay with my back towards him. He puts his arm around me, and begins snoring. He repeats the same act every night.

Ashanti does not want to sleep next to the captain any more. She begins thinking about how she is going to separate from him and sleep somewhere else. Tonight she will be already lying on her own mat, on the floor, at the foot of his bed when he comes in. She hears him coming up the stairs that leads to his chamber. He turns the light on and begins undressing.

Ashanti is acting like she is sleeping while peeking out of one of her eyes. The captain looks over towards his bed and notices Ashanti not there. He then spots her and begins walking towards her. Ashanti closes her eyes anticipating some kind of interaction. He bends down smiles and pats her on the head before climbing in his own bed. Ashanti is relieved and goes into a deep sleep with a smirk on her face.

As time passes by, Ashanti often thinks about home, Mojo, and the village. She envisions herself walking down the path that leads toward the village with animals escorting her and keeping her company throughout her journey. Her visions are usually disrupted by the screams coming from the other villagers that are kept in the belly of the wind catching beast.

Many of my people that have been captured have been dying during this journey. Once they are dead the white men just throw them over board, in pretty much the same way they dispose of their garbage. I often go to the rooms where they are being held captive to help and give attention to the sick and dying. The condition in which they are living, are unlike anything I have ever seen. People are stacked on top of one another. They throw up and even spill their waste right where they lay.

Ashanti helps to save the lives of many of the captives by applying the knowledge that she has learned from Mojo. She persuades the captain to allow the captives to come out the belly of the beast a couple time s a day, to get some fresh air and to move around so they can keep their bodies healthy. Ashanti has been on the ship for a month and little by little she is able to understand the white man's language. She understands more than she can speak.

One day Ashanti overhears one of the men talking to the captain about her. "Captain, that slave of yours should stay on board of the ship permanently; after all, she has been saving many of her peoples by helping to keep them healthy and doctoring on them. This will create more revenue from each voyage; before her appearance on this ship a lot of our profit had just been thrown overboard due to sickness."

Ashanti becomes horrified at what she has just heard. *I know that I have to do something, or else, I will be stuck on this beast for who knows how long. I know I have to work another Mojo on the captain. I have to do it soon, because of what I just heard from that man speaking to the captain. The way the men are speaking I can tell they are getting close to the end of this journey.*

On this particular day she prepares the captain's food like she does on any other day, except this morning it is a little bit different. She pours more than the usual amount of the contents in her pouch in his food. She again recites her incantations as she is mixing the food - "Zooka Mallie"- just like the first time. This time she is anxious and nervous about her "Mojo" having the effect that she wants on the captain. If it does not work she knows that she could be stuck on the ship for life.

Next morning Ashanti hears birds singing. She hasn't heard those sounds in a very long time. She immediately jumps up off her mat and runs to open the door to see land again. She gets a bucket of water and washes herself in anticipation of standing on solid ground. The sailors are moving in a frenzied rush as they all prepare to dock. The ship lines up with the dock and one of the sailors hops off the ship and ties it to a wooden pole rising up from the dock. The captives are being led out of the belly of the ship and line up in front of a wooden ramp that will lead them off the ship. Ashanti gets in line with them in order to proceed off of the ship. As she gets closer to the wooden board leading off the ship, a large arm interposes itself, stopping her from leaving the ship. She looks up and sees the man who was talking to the captain about retaining her on board. He says, "Where do you think you're going?" She points towards the shore. He replies, "I don't think so," and tries to pull her out of the line. Suddenly, two big arms grab him and pull his hand off Ashanti. It is the captain, he tells the sailor, "Let her be. She's going ashore. In fact, I am going to change my cargo all together; no more human cargo on my ship."

He puts his arm around Ashanti and kisses her on the forehead before placing her back in line. He smiles at her as she walks off the ship. The man who tried to stop Ashanti is now confused. To him Ashanti is nothing more than just another slave, a piece of property. He doesn't understand why the captain is showing so much kindness and respect to her. Little does he know that Ashanti knows the art of magic and healing, his captain has been *"Mojoed."*

As Ashanti is led to a barn she notices that there are people who look like her, but are dressed in the same way as the white people. She looks into their eyes attempting to get a response from them but they just turn up their noses, regarding her as less, or even nothing. She is baffled, not being able to understand how her own people can look past her without even acknowledging her presence. One of the white men that was escorting the captives opened a big barn door and the captives are herded into the barn. The barn is not as tight as the big hut Ashanti was kept in, back in her homeland, but it is still a pretty tight space and quite unbearable. Ashanti and her people sit in the barn for four straight days having very little food or water. Other than opening the door to feed them slop, the big barn door is always shut. They get light only through cracks in the wood and at night it gets really dark inside the barn.

In my homeland, people treat animals better than these pale faced people treat us.

On the morning of the fifth day Ashanti is brought to the area where the auction takes place. She is led up four steps onto a platform. She is fully aware of what has happened to the others that have gone before her. A man is speaking so fast that she cannot figure out how the other white men can understand him. Ashanti was next as they led her to the center of the platform. About six or seven men get their hands up showing their interest in having Ashanti. After several bids, there are only two men left taking turns bidding on her. Ashanti is attentively witnessing the whole spectacle, while listening to the fast talking man.

One of the men is short and fat, I don't like the way in which he keeps looking at me as he bids. The other man is tall, muscular, with twinkles in his beautiful blue eyes and yellow hair, just like the sun. He doesn't seem to be like the others. It may be forbidden, but Ashanti feels attracted to this pale skinned man and she hopes he is the one that will take her away. This pale skinned man seems to be very determined to get her at any cost. He begins to look angrily at the short fat man, as he continues to make his bid for Ashanti each time higher and higher.

Ultimately, the fast speaking man slams a stick with a fat head on it. Then the man with yellow hair and twinkles in his eyes smiles at me as another man walks to me and escorts me down from the platform and guides me to him. He holds Ashanti by the hand and they both walk away from the platform. The others continue raising their hands in order to bid for the captives that arrive on the platform after Ashanti.

The man helps me climb onto a cart with big wheels that is pulled by two zebras with no stripes. They are the same type of zebras as the ones in which the white men were sitting on while I was in chains before getting on the wind catching beast. With a flip of the man's wrists the rope that extends from the zebra's mouth incites the zebras to start pulling and we start moving. Little does Ashanti know that she has just been purchased and she is now the property of Thadeus Wellington.

Thadeus is about six feet and two inches tall and weighs about two hundred and thirty pounds. He has blond hair and blue eyes and he is also well built. He doesn't look much older than Ashanti physically, but he surpasses her by ten years. Ashanti, for some reason, doesn't seem to be bothered by the way he has been looking at her all this time. She actually thinks that he is a very handsome man. On the other hand, all the other men who kept staring at Ashanti in that same way, made her feel very uneasy. As they ride, Thadeus keeps undressing the rags that she is wearing off her body with his eyes. He doesn't know what to say to her. He comes from a family of well to do people.

He has had sex with many women, both white and black. He has the gift of being a ladies' man, but for some reason, he just doesn't know what to say to Ashanti. He feels as if he is in front of royalty and actually feels intimidated by her beauty and grace. He begins trying to put a conversation together in his mind. "Maybe I should ask her how was her trip?" he wondered to himself, "No, no, no, that's a dumb question. I got it. Yeah, yeah, I can ask her if she can speak English. That's what I'll ask her." He looks at Ashanti and says, "Um, do you speak English?" Ashanti bashfully puts her head down toward Thadeus and nods yes while drawing her thumb and index fingers close together indicating that she knows only a little bit.

"Oh, that's good cuz' you can keep me company by talkin' to me on our way home." Ashanti gets a bewildered look on her face after she hears the words, "our way home." She does not understand, she thinks to herself, "My home is a long way from here." She nods her head yes rolling her two big brown beautiful eyes, putting her head down on her chest while giving

Thadeus a very innocent bashful look which makes Thadeus feel like he is about to melt in his seat.

"Well, say something. What's your name?"

Ashanti snaps out of her bashfulness, "My name be Ashanti."

"Aish-a-y-ntee, I think that will be hard for me to remember or say. What if I call you Baby Girl? My name is Thadeus Wellington." He reaches out his hand and they shake hands.

It really doesn't go well with Ashanti to be called "Baby Girl," but she rather have that than to hear Thadeus butchering her name again the way he just did. Thadeus looks back at Ashanti and says, "Baby Girl, you and I gonna be just fine." Ashanti clears her throat, "Um, um, where you be takin me, Thththadeus?"

"You are going to my estate. We are in the state of Mississippi and we are going to a town called Bogue Chitto. There are others like you there."

Ashanti points her finger at herself, "Like me?"

"Yes, like you. You are going to be happy there cuz' you're mine."

Ashanti immediately begins to ponder what she has just heard coming out of Thadeus' mouth. Thadeus also tells her, "I just bought you back there at the auction block; I own you."

Ashanti fully understands what Thadeus has just told her. "How can someone be own someone else? That no be right. In my homeland no one owns another."

"You ain't home. This is how we do things in this country." Ashanti puts her head down, not happy with what Thadeus has told her.

Thadeus takes one hand off the reins and lifts Ashanti's face by her chin while looking into her big brown pretty eyes and tells her, "Baby Girl, you don't have to fret none. I'm gonna take good care of you. I feel in my heart there is something special about you."

Ashanti feels much better from what she just heard. There is something about the way Thadeus speaks and looks at Ashanti that makes her feel less uneasy about her predicament.

Chapter VI

Ashanti begins to exude her essence drowning Thadeus in it. It is noticeable that he is going under, by the way he keeps staring at her. The journey hasn't gone too long before they come to a stop in front of two large black gates.

There are two boys holding fire sticks who open the gates to let Thadeus and Ashanti in. They each pull one of the gates open while holding the fire in order to light the way. The entrance is paved with red brick, forming a big U shape. After entering, one can either go left or right. In the center of the U there is green grass, with a young oak tree planted in the middle. On the left side of the U there is a path that leads all the way up to the livery stable, the slave quarters and the fields. On the right side of the U lies the Wellington's mansion.

The mansion is white with six large white columns that extend all the way up, giving the impression that they are holding the top porch and roof. They look like the tusks of giant elephants. There are three gable windows on the roof overseeing everything that comes through the main gate. Underneath the windows there is a long second floor porch incased in black railings. At the bottom of each pillar there are lanterns that light the face of this grand mansion, making it seems as if it is smiling at the observer. Between the two middle posts is the entrance of the house. It has two large glass doors which are framed in black. There are three women waiting at the end of the sidewalk, pretty much as if they already knew that Thadeus and Ashante were coming. Ashanti notices that these women look like her but are not dressed like her. *They dress like the white people and talk like them too. All three of them look at me in a mean, nasty way.*

"Don't pay them no mind, they're just jealous of you. They know I won't be diggin' in them that much cuz' you're here." Thadeus laughs while the three women that are coming to get Ashanti to clean her up don't think it is funny. Thadeus tells them to clean Ashanti up and then bring her to his room. He kisses Ashanti on her forehead, looks her in her eyes and says, "I'll be back directly." He then looks at the three ladies before leaving, "Na' don't y'all hurt my Baby Girl."

The two largest women, who I will later find out are named Bulla and the other MayBell, lead me into a room that has a big wooden bowl full of water. In the mansion, Bulla usually does all the cooking while MayBell does all the washing and they share cleaning duties. One of them is light brown with freckles in her face. The other woman is dark brown with a gap between her top front teeth. They both are pretty and are large women. They begin to wash me in a pretty rough way while holding their noses, as if they smell something very foul. I must smell pretty bad since I haven't bathed thoroughly in weeks. After they scrubbed and washed me, they spray me with a beautiful smelling scent. I now smell like a field of flowers waiting to be embraced by the African sun. The third woman brushes my hair and gives me something to rinse my mouth with. If looks could kill, I would have been dead on the spot. The third woman really gives me a bad eye as though I took her most prized possession. She is actually treating me very rough as she brushes my hair. She digs the brush hard into my scalp, while snatching my head around like a rag doll. I had to turn around and give her a bad look to let her know that I mean business. After Ashanti's gesture, the woman begins to brush Ashanti's hair with more sense. Once again, if looks could kill, Ashanti would be dead right on the spot. *The third woman is not as big as the other two. She actually looks pretty good for her age.* Ashanti is then given a very light robe to wear. *As it touches my skin it feels almost as if I am being touched by a spirit. I am being treated like an African princess.*

The women escort Ashanti up a spiraling staircase. They open the door and instruct Ashanti to lay on a matt that is floating on air. *Before I lay down, they gesture to me to take off the spirit cloth. I don't know why, because I like the way it feels on me. The floating matt is in the middle of four posts that are as big as young trees. I have never laid on a matt as soft as this one. I feel as if I am floating on a cloud.*

Shortly after, Thadeus comes into the room where Ashanti has been lying naked on the floating matt. He begins to kiss her on her lips, down her neck, making her feel in a way that she has never felt before. Just before he gets down to her breasts, he suddenly turns his head and shakes it in disgust.

He has come across her pouch and he doesn't like the way it smells. He gently tries to take it off. Ashanti grabs it, as he continues to unloosen the pouch from her hand; he finally takes it from around her neck. Ashanti stops resisting as Thadeus keeps on kissing her all over her body. He makes passionate love to her on this night and every chance he gets thereafter. Thadeus enjoys every moment he spends with her. Ashanti doesn't have to put a "Mojo" on Thadeus because her loving and essence in itself is his "Mojo." After that night, Thadeus will let Ashanti sleep with him every night.

The next morning Ashanti is awaken by the smell of food. Some of the smells are recognizable, while others are completely foreign to her. She begins to look around for Thadeus and she even yells out his name. Ashanti puts on her robe and runs up to the top of the stair case calling his name. Thadeus comes around the corner, looking up at Ashanti and says, "Baby Girl, here I am. Now you go back into the room. I will be up there directly, ok?" Ashanti nods her head yes and goes back into the room. Thadeus goes up stairs with a tray full of food and two tall glasses full of orange juice. Ashanti is sitting on the matt in a fetal position, with her head resting on her knees. Thadeus pushes her knees down and places the tray over her legs. She voraciously starts devouring the food. She hasn't had much to eat since she left the ship. She was fed very little while she was in the barn waiting to be sold. Thadeus has never asked her if she is hungry, all he has been thinking about is that Ashanti is his main course.

Thadeus looks at Ashanti, "Slow down Baby Girl, there's more food where that came from." Ashanti acts as if she didn't even hear him. She eats as fast as she can because she is very hungry. Thadeus sits down next to her and watches her eat. When she is finished eating Thadeus calls Geechee to come and get the tray. While taking the tray off Ashanti's lap, Geechee gives Ashanti the dirtiest look one can imagine.

Ashanti goes into the bathroom and washes up. When she comes out she already has some clean clothes lying on the bed, which consist of a light grey dress and a white scarf that she covers her hair with. She also walks around bare footed like everyone else. In fact all the women dress this way. Just as she is finishing getting dressed Thadeus steps into the room. "Come on Baby Girl let me show you around the house." He grabs her hand and they start walking out the room heading toward the spiraling stair case. When they reach the bottom of the staircase, they take a right and go into a very large room with a long table and tall chairs standing side by side neatly pushed under the table. There is a big glass object hanging from the ceiling with candles placed around it. Ashanti points at it and asks,

"Thadeus, what that be called?"

"That is a chandelier. We eat here on special occasions like Christmas, birthdays and when ever we have special company. We also have dances in here where people dress up in their finest clothes and dance the night away as the band plays on."

"Thadeus, what be dances?"

"Oh, Baby Girl"

He grabs Ashanti putting his right arm around her waist and holding his left hand on hers, up in the air. Spinning around, Thadeus creates the mood of a dance, "Bum, bum, bum; bum, bum, bum." As Thadeus is twirling her about, she relives in her mind the smell and the rhythm of the music from the many celebrations she was a part of back in her homeland. This makes her heart heavy, sinking into her chest. Ashanti looks at Thadeus with a bewildered look on her face. Thadeus stops dancing wondering why Ashanti is looking at him in such a manner.

"What's wrong?"

"That not be dancin. This be dancin."

Ashanti starts juking and working her body rhythmically to the music from her homeland which is forever stuck in her body, mind and soul.

"I see. Well, we white folks can't dance like that; I see the way y'all dance when we have hoe downs. Y'all black folks really know how to cut a rug."

From the end of that room they walk into another room that has beautiful furniture and paintings. He points at a big painting and says,

"This is a painting of my father."

"Where he be?"

"He died and left the plantation to me."

After leaving that room they walk down a long hall. There are doors which they pass by but he doesn't bother to take Ashanti into those rooms. He opens the third door and they walk into the room.

"Now, this is my library and these are my books."

"What be books?"

"They teach you how to do things or they can tell you a story."

Ashanti grabs a book and opens it, looking at the letters wondering what they might mean.

At the end of the hall is the kitchen where Bulla is cooking. She smiles as Thadeus walks in first; her smile quickly turns into a frown as she sees Ashanti. "This here is the kitchen, this is where ol' Bulla fixes our fiddles." Bulla is facing the stove while stirring something in a pot. Thadeus smacks her on her behind and she jumps a little with a smile from the attention that Thadeus has just given her. They walk out of the kitchen and there are two bedrooms at the corner where they are met by another long hallway. Thadeus points at one of the rooms and says, "Bulla and MayBell share this room and the other one is Geechee's."

Ashanti is glad that Thadeus hasn't told her where her room is because she likes it where she has been sleeping thus far. They begin walking down the long hallway and stop at another room. Thadeus turns to Ashanti stopping her in her tracks. He then puts his hands over her eyes,

"Now Baby Girl, I have a surprise for you."

He leads Ashanti into the room and then he suddenly stops. He slowly takes his hands off her eyes. To Ashanti's horror it is a giant animal with big claws and teeth staring at her. It makes her jump and her heart feels as if it is going to bust through her chest. She immediately runs behind a laughing Thadeus seeking his protection. He slowly slides down on the floor laughing as hard as he possibly can. Ashanti slides down with him in horror. He gets up off the floor to console her.

"Baby Girl, that bear is dead. My father killed him and we had it stuffed. Ah, Baby Girl, you're trembling."

Ashanti continues to look around the room seeing the heads of other animals mounted on walls.

Thadeus puts his arms tightly around Ashanti's waist making her feel safe. He points to a long green table with rails around it. He grabs a stick and gets two balls from one of the holes that are placed around the table. He puts both balls on the table as he bends over the table with the stick in his hands, pointing it at the white ball. He pushes forward and moves the stick back and forth through his fingers saying, "Baby Girl, this here's a pool table." He hits the white ball making it hit one of the colored balls, that goes into one of the holes. After knocking the ball into the hole he stands up in a boastful stance saying, "Baby Girl, maybe I'll teach you how to play one day. By the way, this right here is called the game room. I come here to relax and unwind after a long day." Thadeus walks out the room first and Ashanti quickly rubs the teeth and the claws of the bear and smiles at it before leaving. They leave that room and walk by more doors for which Thadeus doesn't bother to show Ashanti what is behind them. When they get to the end of the hallway, they are back at where they started, which is in front of the double spiraling staircases.

Ashanti doesn't have to sleep in the slave quarters, and that makes Geechee, Bulla and MayBell very unhappy. Geechee is the woman who was brushing Ashanti's hair with roughness and disdain when Ashanti first got to the mansion. Thadeus has slept with all three of his slave women; Geechee has always been his main mistress until Ashanti showed up.

Geechee is a little taller than Ashanti with reddish brown hair. She has the same curvy body like Ashanti but she is much older. Her lips are full and her breast are still firm although she has already had a few children by Thadeus but those pregnancies have done nothing to destroy her naturally beautiful physique. *She is somewhat similar to me in her physique and cuteness but she doesn't have Sheba in her the way I do.* As time goes on, she still doesn't talk to Ashanti, she only keeps on giving Ashanti deadly looks, like wishing she could kill her. In fact, all three of these women keep on giving Ashanti the same type of look every time they see her because Ashanti has not done any work, only pleasuring Thadeus. Ashanti wants to be Geechee's friend since she doesn't feel the same way about Geechee as Geechee feels about her. She also wants to be Geechee's friend because she considers Geechee as an older version of herself. In her mind, Ashanti feels like Geechee is an older sister that she has never had.

One day, as Geechee is cleaning one of the big silver serving trays, Ashanti asks her, "Geechee, don't you miss our homeland?" Geechee slowly turns her head around toward Ashanti like a snake with its victim coiled, squeezing the life out of it and ready to swallow it up.

"I ain't from where you're from. I'm from Louisiana. I'm creole; I speak French as well as English. I no be one of y'all Ubadoos from Africa."

"I no be no Ubadoo. I be Ashanti!"

Geechee looks at Ashanti while rolling her eyes, "Well, anyway, yes, I think bout me homeland Louisiana with it weepin willas that sway back and forth when the wind picks up just befo it be getin' ret' to rain. My masta let us be, us do what we wanna, long as business was taken care of in da house. I had a kinky red colored hair boy from da next plantation over. He be few years older den me. He was tall and built like an oak tree and hung like Dingo down there."

"How is Dingo down there?," comes to Ashanti's mind.

"Thadeus is ok as far as how he treats us, but de rest of de plantations 'round here treat us like animals," continued Geechee. "Don't wanna get sold to somewhere else cuz' it be turible."

Geechee snaps out of her reminiscing daze and again stares at Ashanti in a nasty way. "See." Geechee keeps on telling Ashanti, "Thadeus is not the daddy of all' my baby chaps. He not do me like Dingo, cuz' he go real deep. Many a nights I slip out back ta get dingoed; he be my sleep medicine when I cane't fall asleep. I glad you be here so you can get short served by Thadeus," Geechee starts laughing as she is still saying these last words.

Dingo is one of Thadeus' slaves that works the fields. He is about six feet and six inches tall weighs about two hundred and sixty pounds of pure hard man. He has thick juicy lips with a boyish smile. He has no hair on his head or his face. They call him "Dingo" because he is from the Mandingo tribe in Africa.

"I have seen him only passing by," utters Ashanti, "How many of us be here Thadeus got?"

"There 'bout twenty five or thirty of us," replies Geechee. "Some of us be here befo Thadeus start making babies with us. His daddy left some a dem here fo' he died."

"Why they be callin' you Geechee? What's a Geechee?"

"I be not know. Why y'all be askin all dese questions fo?"

Ashanti bashfully puts her head down while still looking at Geechee, playing with her fingers behind her back. She says, "Me just askin."

"When my masta's gone to die his son, who be de one dat get masta's land. When he get it, he begin sellin' erythang; Thadeus be de one who get me. He be at an auction while visitin in Na O'lean."

Just like Ashanti, Geechee is very sexy and shapely. That's why Thadeus had to have her.

" After he buy me and take me here and we get in front of the mansion where MayBell and Bulla be waitin," continues Geechee. "To dem he yell out, come meet my Geechee gal. They all look at me face crossed, rollin dey eyes. Dem no like me much cuz' masta don't do dem not much no mo.' He be wantin' dis all da time," as Geechee says this, she pats her stuff between her legs.

"What do Geechee be meanin?" insists Ashanti.

"I done told ya, I don't know, cuz' dat be some Mississippi talk, me be from Louisiana"

"I ain't be here fo' dat long. Dat's why I be askin all dese questions,"

The comment about Geechee replacing MayBell and Bulla in order to satisfy Thadeus' sexual preferences tickles Geechee so that she goes on laughing as she keeps on shinning the silver serving tray. She puts the tray back into the hutch of the cabinet where the silver is kept. She looks back at Ashanti and smiles before gracefully slithering out of sight. Ashanti doesn't understand why Geechee is laughing at the fact that Thadeus now chooses Ashanti over her. Ashanti now thinks that she should have told Geechee that, while patting herself on her own stuff between her legs. By doing so, she would have wiped Geechee's silly grin off her face. Geechee has a way about herself that will make any man want to have her. The way she talks and walks along with her juicy lips is practically impossible for a man to resist. Ashanti now understands why Thadeus had taken Geechee, and at the same time she realizes why he is now replacing Ashanti for Geechee. She probably looks the same way Geechee used to look during her younger days. To Thadeus, Ashanti probably is newer and improved. Geechee is the main maid and the one who really runs the house.

One afternoon a group of men who owned plantations and businesses, come by to talk business with Thadeus. Ashanti continuously exudes herself, even when she doesn't realize it. She wants to make sure that Thadeus doesn't stop at any of his old watering holes; she wants to make sure that she is keeping his loving just for herself. When she walks by the men, one of them grabs her arm and begins rubbing her chest with his other hand. Geechee is standing at the corner of the room watching everything. The name of the man is Mr. Gilbert Poole. He owns a livestock feed business in town. Thadeus knew him ever since they were young chaps. He is the same age as Thadeus's older brother. In fact, the two of them have been friends since childhood. Ashanti starts fighting back by pulling away from him. Thadeus hears Ashanti's voice and he immediately runs inside to see what the problem is.

Ashanti has kicked Mr. Poole in the shin. Mr. Poole throws her down and is ready to strike her when Thadeus grabs his arm. Geechee starts thinking about what is going to happen to Ashanti for having hit a white man. "She done did it now!" screams Geechee. She done hit a white man; she gonna get some lashes now!"

Mr. Poole tells Thadeus, "Yo niggra hit me, she needs some lashes!"

"Now Gilbert, you been roughing her up trying to get some. I knows ya, and this one, I ain't sharing. Now, if you want to sow your oats, Geechee's is yonder in the kitchen!"

When Geechee overhears Thadeus offering her services to appease Mr. Poole she backs away, not too far, where she cannot hear the conversation in the room but far enough where she can run away and hide in case Mr. Poole takes Thadeus up on his offer. Geechee does not want to be touched again by that greasy, fat bastard.

"You can't have this one," says Thadeus.

"Naw, I'll pass on Geechee" replies Mr. Poole. "cuz' the last time I had a hold of her it was like if a train had gone through her."

Geechee's face frowns as she hears Mr. Poole's reply to Thadeus.

Ashanti looks at Mr. Poole as if to say, "My baby told you." as Mr. Poole turns as red as an apple. She looks up into Thadeus' eyes and rubs herself on him as if she is drying off on him like Sheba and says.

"Baby, I be goin upstairs and lay down."

"Ok Baby Girl, I'll be up there in a little bit."

Ashanti overhears Mr. Poole talking to Thadeus. She can hear the man who just tried to rape her saying, "You done been ruined by that girl. You can't allow that girl to sleep with you every night like she is yo wife or somethin. She belongs in the back with the rest of yo slaves. I heard you paid a pretty penny for her. What kinda work can she do?"

Thadeus does not answer.

"Ah, I see," Continues Mr. Poole, "That Poontang got yo nose wide open and that cat got your tongue. You better put her in her place cuz' if the rest of the plantation owners hear 'bout this, you will be black balled from all the functions that men of our caliber attend. You and yo damn brother are being ruined by these damn nigras."

Thadeus has an older brother named Douglas who has a smaller plantation of his own. Their father did not leave the plantation to him because he likes to party and gamble too much. Their father also liked partying and gambling as well but he never allowed it to take anything away from his establishment. Thadeus, on the other hand, has never indulged in partying, gambling or drinking, but these vices seem to be in his brother's blood. Ever since their fathers death Douglas has gotten his life together and Thadeus loaned him some money so he could buy a small estate a few miles away from his. In a town called Springfield.

A serious Thadeus replies to Mr. Poole, "I'm gonna take care of it. Don't worry!"

"I ain't worrying, y'all betta fix that soon." states Mr. Poole.

"Let us be on our way."

The three gentlemen walk out the door. Thadeus in the meantime, goes up to talk to Ashanti. "Now, Baby Girl, you can't go around hitting white men." As he is talking, Ashanti takes the sheet off her and starts fanning her legs back and forth.

"And I'm gonna have to build you yo own cabin in the back. Now Baby Girl, I ain't playing with you." Thadeus's voice starts to get distorted as Ashanti starts peeling her clothes off. Thadeus can barely contain his composure after smelling her pheromones being fanned in his direction as Ashanti slowly flaps her legs making Thadeus' nature soar. As Thadeus lies on top of her, he asks, "By the way, what work can you do 'round here?" Ashanti pulls him close to her lips and muffles any word that may come out of his mouth.

Next morning Thadeus wakes up, rolls over, but Ashanti is not there. He jumps out of the bed calling her, "Baby Girl, Baby Girl!" He runs into the kitchen, where Bulla is preparing breakfast.

"Bulla, you seen Baby Girl?"

"She told me she heard one of the milk cows calling her; that be over an hour ago,"

Thadeus runs back upstairs and puts on his overalls and boots and leaves heading for the barn. When he gets there he finds Ashanti easing a calf out of its mother. Old Sam, as well, witnesses Ashanti working her magic as she delivers the calf. Sam walks over to Thadeus, "Masta, I never seen anythang like dat in all my days."

"What you mean?"

"Well, it seems like she's talkin to da baby's mama, and the baby come right out. She ain't need no help from me. She just tell me to hold the cows head to comfort her. Masta, you'n got one." Thadeus looks back at Sam smiling, "I know."

Ashanti has a towel in which she is wiping the fluids off and simultaneously talking to the new born calf. "Ashanti, got it; you goan be just fine." She lays the calf down next to its mother, they both stand up and it starts suckling from its mother's nipple after staggering to it's feet.

Ashanti grabs another towel and wipes her hands off while patting the mother cow on the head saying, "Na you 'n goan take care of our baby, ya hear?" The cow nods her head as if she understands what Ashanti is saying. Thadeus looks at Ashanti saying, "Ashanti, I was worried about when that cow was going to deliver. I was thinking about how much money I was going to have to pay the veterinarian just to deliver that baby calf."

"You ain't got to give him no mo' dat cuz' I'z here now."

Thadeus pulls Ashanti close to him and Ashanti smiles displaying her pretty white teeth and her well defined dimples. As Ashanti stands up he notices that Ashanti is wearing his overalls and has a pair of his boots on, with the bottoms of her pants cuffed up and a straw hat tilted to the side exposing her white scarf, with a piece of straw in the corner of her mouth. "Girl what you got on?" as he twirls her around to see what she is wearing. Her butt really sticks out because she put the overalls over her dress. "I don't like the way my booty is sticking out back there." Ashanti unclips the overalls and pulls her dress out clipping them back up under her dress. "Now that's more like it. Though I aint used to seeing no women with no briches on." Ashanti smiles and says, "Get use to it." "You going to be mighty hot in all that." "As long as me have some wadah in me my sweat be keepin' me cool." Ashante only wears the boots when she goes into town. Other than that she is bare footed. Even when Thadeus gets her overalls her size she still cuffs up the bottom, which has the boys on the plantation doing the same. Thadeus takes Ashanti on a ride around his plantation so she can give him her opinion on the dynamics of the plantation and discuss how to operate it better, because she is always thinking. Ashante does not say anything about his plantation because she has something else on her mind. On their way back to the mansion she asks Thadeus a question,

"I be thinkin' I be have to move out cho place soon, right?"

"Yeah, that's right." Thadeus is glad Ashanti is the one posing this question since he doesn't know how, or has the heart to tell her that she needs to move into her own place.

"Den, let me show you where I want to live. You'n fix it the way I wont it."

Thadeus looks at Ashanti, "Ok Baby Girl, you got that."

They walk about 100 yards behind the mansion just as the path curves going towards the livery stable, barn and slave quarters. She stops Thadeus and says "I wont ta live right here," She begins drawing in the dirt with a stick how she wants her house built. "I kinda understand how you want it; we will get back to it later." As they get closer to the mansion, Geechee is standing in the back doorway waving for Thadeus to come in. Geechee tells Thadeus, "Thadeus the licka and thang man be in de game room ta see ya." The so called Licka man is the local peddler who sells just about everything, from alcoholic beverages to spoons and forks. Thadeus purchases cooking sherry and moon shine from the peddler. Ashanti watches as money exchanges from one hand to the other. The man gathers up his goods and Geechee escorts him to the door. Ashanti asks, "What be dat you give that man and what dat he give you?" This is cooking sherry, the girls use this to cook with and this is what they call White lightenin.'" "What be White lightenin?" Well it's what we drink that makes us feel real good. You will see what it does to ya when they have the ho down after harvest." He pinches her cheek as he is speaking.

"What was that you gave the man for the white lightenin'? " We use these bills and change to purchase goods." Ashanti holds bills and plays with the coins in her hand: quarters, nickels, dimes and pennies.

"What did y'all use in your home land to purchase goods?" "We be usin gold, cowry shells, work, cattle and crops to get what we be needin.'" We call that bartering here in America." She asks Thadeus what each currency is worth and Thadeus tells her. "Well let me keep dis money so we can have it when we need to pppurchase one mo ginn." Thadeus reluctantly lets her have the money thinking that her people don't know anything about the value of money. "Here Baby Girl you can have it." Ashanti takes the money and puts it in one of her pockets. "Now I got to go on a run and I will be back by dinner." Geechee watching all that just transpired is heated. Thadeus has never done such a thing with her. Ashanti disappears after Thadeus leaves. While dinner is being served Ashanti pops up out of nowhere handing Thadeus a piece of paper. He puts his fork down and unfolds the paper. He shakes his head and smiles as he looks at Ashanti.

"Baby Girl, you something else, you done made a blueprint of how you want yo place to be built. Well, I'll be." She bashfully rolls her big brown eyes, putting her head down to her chest displaying her dimples and her pearly white teeth. She has her hands clasped behind her back and her feet in a pigeon toed stance. Thadeus grabs Ashanti and puts her in his lap.

"Well Baby Girl, seeing that you know what you want, I'm gonna build it for ya." Ashanti kisses Thadeus on his cheek and takes a piece of meat off his plate. She lets him bite a piece before putting the rest in her mouth. They both smile at each other while chewing. The other women in the house, Geechee, MayBell and Bulla are very mad after witnessing what has just happened in their presence.

Next morning Ashanti wakes up from noises coming from behind the mansion. She jumps off the bed and runs to the second floor back porch. She sees all the unpaid workers from Thadeus's plantation working on her house. Ashanti calls Thadeus as she waves her arms frantically trying to get his attention. He looks at her and smiles, then turns around to continue directing his workers. Ashanti runs to the bathroom to wash up and get dressed before going out to help in the construction of her future home. As she passes by Bulla and MayBell, both roll their eyes, since all they have is a small room in the corner of the mansion. They are livid because Ashanti will have her own home built. Ashanti's house is being built a hundred yards behind the mansion and a few hundred yards away from the slave quarters.

When Ashanti arrives at the construction site she gives Thadeus a big hug and a kiss. She turns away from Thadeus and immediately starts directing the workers on how she wants her house to be built. She looks at Thadeus and yells out,

"This not be right. The fire place goes here, I be wontin three bedrooms back dair."

"Now listen, Baby Girl, I'll let you do this cuz' you ain't going to aggravate

43

me," exclaims Thadeus angrily handing the blue print to Ashanti and marches back towards the mansion. Ashanti smiles as she unwrinkles the blue print for her house. He turns to Ashanti and yells, "You got three days to finish yo' house cuz' they got to get back to the going ons on this plantation.

Ya heard?," yells Thadeus, "Yes Thadeus."

Chapter VII

The work on her house is going smoothly. Everyone who comes in contact with Ashanti seems to instantly get along with her. Thadeus watches, as Ashanti directs the men building her house. He notices how each one of them, change their body language as they interact with her; pretty much in the same manner the young men would be influenced by her presence back in her old country. Ashante's essence has the men working extra hard to build her house. Dingo seems to be the one that is most captured by Ashanti's presence and beauty. He loves to take his shirt off at lunch time and pour water down his body from the top of his head letting it cascade down his muscular body. Ashanti enjoys watching him doing this. She thinks to herself, "What a fine specimen of a black man."

At the end of the third day the house is almost complete. All that it needs now is the shingles on the roof. Dingo walks up to Ashanti, "Miss lady, it was good helpin'y'all to build yo house." He takes her hand and kisses it. Ashanti bats her eyes in a bashful seductive way. With her hand still in Dingo's she replies, "Thanks ya to Dingo." They both feel eyes being laid on them and they both feel a chill running through their bodies. They turn around and look back towards the mansion where they see Geechee and Thadeus standing and looking at them. Geechee is standing about ten feet in front of Thadeus with her arms crossed and a mean look on her face as she stares down at Dingo. Thadeus ears are red as freshly drawn blood as he looks at Ashanti with a hard face. Thadeus yells out, "Dingo, now y'all head back to yo quarters and get ready for tamara cuz' we got some catchin'up to do." Dingo, with his hard strong body, cowers to Thadeus' command.

"Yessa boss; right away"

Dingo turns around ready to go back to his quarters. He sneaks a final look of admiration at Ashanti and she does the same before she completely turns around and goes in the opposite direction. After he takes a few steps, Dingo looks back at Geechee to see if she still has a disappointing look on her face. She is still standing in the same hard stance that she was in when he first looked at her. Thadeus starts walking toward Ashanti, who feels guilty for flirting with Dingo. When he reaches Ashanti she comes up to him and wraps her arms around him and looks into his eyes saying, "Baby, see, we be almost done." Thadeus doesn't hug Ashanti, he just looks past her showing no emotions. Ashanti immediately grabs Thadeus's arm and pulls him to the front of the main entrance of her house to show him what it looks like inside. Thadeus pulls his arm back and snatches his hand out of Ashanti's saying, "You ain't got to pull me, I know where the front dowe is."

As they walk in the house Ashanti begins to show Thadeus the house, always staying a few steps away from him so he can feel her coldness reciprocating his earlier actions toward her. She knows that Thadeus can't help but love her. She knows that he can't resist putting his hands on her firm ripe body. As they walk around, Thadeus tries to get closer to her but she always manages to remain a few steps away. He can no longer take not being able to touch her, so he suddenly steps to her and grabs her.

"Baby Girl, you trying to avoid me," turning her face to face with him. She squirms, trying to get out of his grasp.

"Now Thadeus, you'n pulled way from me and actin' not nice fo' no reason. I ain't did you nothin'."

"I know this! You betta not give away none of my lovin."

Ashanti stops squirming and looks into Thadeus's eyes. "I will neva give nonna yo' stuff to nobody, ya hear me." Ashanti reassures Thadeus that she is all his. They both embrace, with love in their eyes. She continues showing her house to Thadeus. They walk outside and she points to her roof.

"Thadeus, all we's got left is da roof, so no wadah be not comin'in."

"Well Ashanti, it will take only a few guys to finish. I will send them down in the morning. We have a lot of work to do in the fields. Don't want to fall behind cuz' time is money. When you get tired of playing 'round down here come to the house cuz' we got somewhere to go."

Ashanti nods her head yes, "I' be dar direca." Thadeus turns around saying, "And by the way, Dingo won't be one of them sent to help you." Ashanti shrugs her shoulders as if to say, "Whatever."

When Thadeus leaves and is out of sight, Dingo comes out of the bushes wide eyed, weary of Thadeus's return. He crouches as he tip toes to Ashanti and whispers, "Baby Girl, I just want chu to know I be fillin' a might good when me be 'round ya."

"I'z the same, Dingo."

"I know masta not want me 'round you no mo,' but 'morra be the last day in da fields. Next day atta, dat be free day, den come God day. I be seein' you on God day."

"What be free day, Dingo?"

"Well, on dat day we not do dat much work we be tendin' to and fixen da tools dat we's need to work in da fields wit."

Ashanti smiles as she reaches out her hand to shake his. "Dingo my name not be Baby Girl my name be Ashanti."

"Ok, Ashanti."

He smiles and bends down, sneakily cowering as he disappears into the woods.

Ashanti must have really had a strong effect on Dingo for him to be risking the grave consequences that he would face if he got caught disobeying Thadeus's orders. As a slave owner Thadeus is pretty liberal in the treatment of his slaves but there are certain behaviors and actions that he will not tolerate. If any of those behaviors or actions are committed, it would be considered a violation of his laws. If any violations do occur, the penalty would certainly be severe.

Ashanti has a warm feeling coming over her as she turns around and walks up the stairs of her new home. She walks up three steps to a long porch that is covered by a roof that is held by three poles on each side. When one walks into her front door, there is a small sectioned room that will become the kitchen, with many shelves to the far right of it. From the outside, one would think the house to be small, but it is sort of an optical illusion because once you look inside the house, it is actually huge. Ashanti looks on the inside of her house, imagining how it will look once it is furnished. She used the inside of Thadeus's house as a scale model for how she wants hers to be.

I want a table with eight chairs under it. I want a mantle over the fire place with objects that I think are beautiful. In my kitchen, I want all my shelves filled with herbs to cook and heal with.

As she is saying this she waves her hand up and down, as if she can already see the herbs there. She opens the door to the first bedroom. *I want a big soft bed with pretty covers on it. I also want fancy candle lights all over the walls.* As she says this she twirls around pointing at the exact spots where she wants the lamps to be. Suddenly she hears someone calling, "Baby Girl!" She snaps out of her day dreaming by Thadeus's beckoning call. She runs to the porch and shuts the door behind her. She yells out, "I'z a comin'," as she jogs toward Thadeus.

When she reaches Thadeus he puts his arm around her neck and allows it to drape accross her chest. "Baby Girl, we're going for a buggy ride."

"Where we be goin' Thadeus?"

"Now, don't you worry yo' pretty little head, just take the ride with daddy."

Ashanti smiles as Thadeus helps her into the carriage. Thadeus climbs up on his side and grabs the reins and pops them on the horse's behind making him move. As the horse pull out of the gate, Ashanti lays her head on Thadeus' shoulder. "I don't know what you done did to me girl, but you got me feeling mighty fine," recites Thadeus in a confessing tone. "All I do is think about you and when I'm around you I can't keep my hands off you."

Ashanti looks at Thadeus with her big brown eyes, "You'n makin' me feel de same way."

Another buggy is riding in the opposite direction and Thadeus tips his hat to the man and woman as they pass. The man in the other carriage does the same, except they have a look of shock on their faces. Thadeus wonders about their reaction to his greeting. Then it hits him, he is riding with Ashanti as if she is a white woman.

He clears his throat, "Ummm, Baby Girl, white people have a funny way of thinking."

"What dat be Thadeus?"

"Well, uh, we white folks ain't supposed to be showing no affection to nigras in public."

Before Thadeus finishes his thought Ashanti says, "Befo dey pass one mo', ginn' I be off you. Baby Girl no wanna cause Thadeus no fuss." Thadeus pulls Ashanti close to him and kisses her on her forehead.

"That's my Baby Girl."

They continue to ride as the sun begins to set. Somehow, they end up back in front of Thadeus's house. All Thadeus did was go on a circular route around the plantation that has brought them back to the front gates.

The two boys with lanterns open the gates wide allowing them to come in. Thadeus pulls in front of the house and gets out of the carriage. He comes to the other side and helps Ashanti down. A black man, who has been sitting and waiting outside, gets in the buggy and pulls off. Thadeus grabs Ashanti and puts her in front of him. He covers her eyes when they get close to the back door of the mansion they continue walking in the direction of Ashanti's house.

As they approach Ashanti's house, lights can be seen coming out of its windows. They climb up the stairs coming to a stop right in front of the main door.

"Now Baby Girl, I'm going to take one of my hands off your eyes. Now, you have to keep 'em shut."

He opens the door and ushers Ashanti across the threshold. He finally takes his hands completely off her eyes. "Now you can open your eyes," says Thadeus. Ashanti's eyes take a few moments before they come back into focus. They have been closed for so long and now they are suddenly bombarded by so many bright lights in her house. There are candles in fancy fixtures all around the room. Straight opposite of Ashanti and Thadeus sits a long table with eight chairs under it. Not of the same elegance as the one in the mansion, but fitting and in good taste for the style of Ashanti's dwelling. Thadeus then leads her to see the mantel over the fire place in which it is aw inspiring to her. He has taken some of the figurines from his own mantel and has also bought other knick knacks, which were placed on her mantel piece. She gets very happy when she sees among the artifacts the pouch that Mojo made for her back in her homeland.

They go into the kitchen where Thadeus has put plates and empty jars on the shelves, and spoons and forks in the little drawers. He backs up with her in front of him leading her into her bedroom. He then nudges the door open with his foot. There is a beautiful soft looking bed with long bed posts around it. Ashanti turns around and faces Thadeus. "Thadeus, you be de keepa o' me dreams." She pulls him toward her and they flop down on the bed, making passionate love all night.

Next morning Thadeus gets up and goes to the mansion without awakening Ashanti. He later comes back and slaps her on her behind making her jump up rubbing her butt with a confused look on her face. Thadeus laughs because he has startled Ashanti out of her sleep.

"Why you be doin'dat Thadeus?" Ashanti exclaims as she rubs her butt.

"Get on up Baby Girl; I got to show you the lay of the land again. This time I want some feedback on how I'm running thangs."

"Ok Thadeus, can chu not wake me dat way?"

"Ok Baby Girl, no more smacks on the butt to get you up."

Ashanti gets up and gets dressed and then meets Thadeus outside of her house where he is sitting on a horse. Ashanti steps down from the porch and Thadeus grabs her by the arm and pulls her up on the horse in front of him. Ashanti turns around and looks at Thadeus,

"Thadeus, I be wantin' me own horse."

"Baby Girl, you don't know nothing about ridin' no horses."

"Now, do ya?" says Thadeus. Ashanti replies with a pouty mouth while crossing her arms., "I be wontin' me own."

"Ok Baby Girl, let's go see Sam so he can saddle you up one."

They ride over to the livery stable where Sam stands as he watches them arrive. Sam begins saddling up a horse for Ashanti.

"Masta, you sure you want me doin' dat? Has she eva rode befo?" asks Sam in a hesitant tone. Thadeus shrugs his shoulders and motions for Sam to go ahead and saddle up the horse. Ashanti stands next to the horse stroking her mane while looking into her big 'round eyes. "Thadeus, what be she name?"

Before Thadeus can respond Sam speaks out, "Her name be Ann; dat's what I call her." Ashanti looks back into the horse's eyes, "My name be Ashanti, and we go be good friends." Sam helps Ashanti up on the horse and gives the reins to Thadeus. Thadeus leads Ashanti on horseback, slightly behind him as they begin to tour his property. They ride inside of his property and point to landmarks to show where his land ends. "You see yonder where that big boulder on the other side of my lake is, that is where my land ends." They continue to ride, "You see where the cotton field ends, about a hundred yards on the other side, I own." They continue to ride, "You see, Baby Girl, where the collard's green and the corn ends, that is my land also."

They come up to a bunch of cows with young boys herding them out to pasture.

"They be dem two boys that be holdin' dem lanterns at da gate at night?" asks Ashanti.

"Yes indeed. Got to start workin' them young so that they can get used to it, because that is what they will be doin' for the rest of their days." Ashanti looks at Thadeus as if he has just said something wrong.

"Of course, when they get too old we have to send them to pastures, like we send an old race horse."

As they pass the two gate keepers both boys smile and tip their broke down straw hats at Ashanti.

"Sam be gettin' too old too; when he be goin' out to pastures?" Ashanti inquires.

"Sam got a good ten, fifteen years before that happens."

"What be collard greens?"

"We plant that to feed the livestock."

"Why you be havin corn and collard green by each uda, and cotton on the end? Cotton be in da midda of corn and collard green; dey grow mo' betta dat way."

Thadeus' mind begins running and thinking about what Ashanti just said. "Well, I have neva thought of that. I will let you direct where all the crops be planted next year."

"I'za do dat fo you Thadeus. I'an show you howz to get de all out of cho crops," Thadeus smiles at Ashanti, "I know you will, Baby Girl; I know you will."

They continue to ride and Ashanti is mesmerized by all the property Thadeus owns. They end up at the slave quarters, which houses most of the inhabitants of the plantation. There are small cabins side by side and across from each other. There are people sitting on porches whittling gardening tools and children playing about. As Thadeus passes, the people stop in their tracks. The men take their hats off as if Thadeus is royalty. They smile and wave at Ashanti as well.

"Who dey be, Thadeus?"

"They are all my slaves. I own all of them."

Ashanti is shocked. *How can one man own this many people?* Ashanti ponders. *I don't understand how my people allow themselves to be owned by one man. Dingo is a lot bigger and stronger than Thadeus; he could break him in half if he wanted to. Thadeus is a big man but he is soft when compared to Dingo. We outnumber him. How can he own us with such ease?*

"Thadeus, why ain't dey workin today?"

"Today is Saturday, which they call free day. They don't have to work today. This day they fix and mend tools to get ready for Monday. If we were behind in our work we would have to work on Saturday, but that doesn't happen very often. I let them off on weekends. I think you have to do that to keep up the moral of your slaves. You get more out of them if you do that. A lot of plantations work their slaves everyday if needed. I don't do that. Sunday is the day of rest, God's day. I learned from my father, never to work yo slaves on Sunday; let them have a dose of the Good Book on that day. You will see cuz' you will be with yo people tomorrow. You will be able to meet the rest of them."

"Thadeus, what be God?"

"Well, God is who made the heavens and the earth and me and you."

"Oh, you be meanin' Omare and Obatalá; and Shangó and Ganaub?"

Thadeus turns around and looks at Ashanti with a befuddled look on his face. "I don't know a damn thang 'bout what you talkin' 'bout. Don't talk bout that Hoodoo, Voodoo shit 'round me. Ya heard?" Ashanti puts her head down and nods yes.

When Ashanti picks her head back up Dingo comes into focus and Ashanti begins to smile. Thadeus turns around and looks at Dingo, which erases Dingo's smile, as he shamefully and humbly cowers at Thadeus's presence. Thadeus quickly turns back toward Ashanti, which erases her smile, dropping her head again. Thadeus drops Ashanti's reins as he talks to Dingo. Ashanti picks up the reins and slaps the side of the horse and she takes off towards her home. Thadeus scratches his head wondering how Ashanti was able to ride the horse without ever riding one before. He then slaps his horse trying to catch up with Ashanti.

When he arrives, Ashanti is off her horse, leading her to Sam. Ashanti hands Sam the reins and starts walking back towards her house. Thadeus arrives shortly after. As he hands his reins to Sam, Sam looks at him, "Thadeus, you be a good teacher, to show that gal how to ride so quickly." Sam has a baffled look on his face, in a daze, letting the words slowly and softly leak out of his mouth.

"I didn't teach her."

Thadeus sees Baby Girl at a distance and begins calling her. "Baby Girl, Baby Girl, wait up." Ashanti continues to walk as if she did not hear him; still upset for having been scolded for introducing Thadeus to her Gods. Ashanti goes in her house slamming the door behind her. Thadeus is not far behind, as he hastily begins to trot to get there quicker. He walks through the door and Ashanti is standing at the window with her arms crossed, pouting. Thadeus eases up behind her.

"Thadeus, I just be tellin' chu what I know." Thadeus grabs Ashanti and turns her around, and looks her in the eyes. "It's not chu, it's you. Say you."

"Ya,ya,ya, you."

"Much better, I was just raised a little bit different from you. If you call out who brought you here to me, then I'll thank them to." He grabs her by the arm and pulls her to the porch looking up in the sky. "I thank whoever brought her to me." He turns around to her and looks into her big brown eyes. "Is that alright now?" Ashanti smiles, batting her thick eyelashes at Thadeus, "That be right now, Thadeus." Little does Thadeus know that he has just embraced Ashanti's essence. He kisses her and ushers her back in the house.

The morning of Ashanti's third Sunday begins with a knock on her door. She rubs her eyes and gets out of bed to open the door. When she opens it she has to cover her eyes, shielding them from the bright glare of the Mississippi sun. To Ashanti's surprise it is Geechee, Bulla and MayBell at the door. They stand there smiling, dressed up in clothes that they don't normally wear, or should we say, their "Sunday best." Geechee speaks first, "Baby Girl, we here to take ya to hear words from the Good Book."

"We be sangin, clappin and shoutin' on this here day," adds Bulla. MayBell nods yes, giving Ashanti an inviting smile. Geechee hands Ashanti some nice clothes to wear. Ashanti smiles, grabs them and turns around and goes in her house. She quickly turns back and opens the door. "I'z not wont y'all to stay out dair, come own in. Set down, I be cleaned up and goan wit' y'all direca. Y'all be liken my house. Their smiles loosen as they look around Ashanti's baby mansion.

"We be the one dat did all the fixin' 'round here while ya be on y'all litta' ride," says Geechee as she stands up to re-familiarize herself with her work. "I don't know what you'n be doin' to Thadeus, but you show got he nose wide open." MayBell laughs, "She must have some o' dat Voodoo on she stuff, got Thadeus goin' crazy. I need some o' dat put on my stuff to make him be licken' me again, cuz' it be a long time since he give me a cleanin." They all laugh as Ashanti is getting dressed. Ashanti is enjoying the comradery of her fellow Thadeus' women.

Ashanti has a long gown that makes her walk funny because she is not used to wearing it. She usually wears a dress just past her knees over her overalls like Thadeus wears. The three ladies pop their umbrellas to shade themselves from the hot late morning Mississippi sun. As they come around the corner of the field that is shared by a patch of woods, they see a big oak tree. Under the oak tree are all of the unpaid inhabitants of Thadeus's plantation. The elderly are sitting on chairs that were brought out from their houses, and some sit on the ground, and the rest stand up. Sam the blacksmith stands in front of everyone with his long black robe and the Bible in his hand, resting against his side. The crowd parts like the Red Sea as Ashanti, Geechee, MayBell and Bulla pass through. It slowly closes as they pass. When they are just about up to Sam, he waves an arm towards a bench where he wants them to be seated. Sam waves his arms and his hands downward, signaling everyone to sit down.

Sam places the Bible on a stand that looks like it was carved out of a single block of wood. He adjusts his black robe that he wears over his "Sunday clothes." He wipes sweat from his forehead with a white handkerchief, caused by the hot midday Mississippi's sun. A child brings him a cup and a wooden pitcher filled with cold water from the well. The child pours him a cup of water and Sam drinks it. He then opens his Bible while clearing his throat, and begins to read. *Now, these are the names of the children of Israel, which came into Egypt; every man in his household came with Jacob: Reuben, Ismael, Levi, Judah, Issachar, Zebulon and Benjamin.* As he speaks, he gets all the attention of his captured congregation that seems to lean forward so not to miss a single word out of Sam's mouth.

After he says a few verses, he explains to his congregation what they mean. *Now arose a new king over Egypt, which knew not Joseph. Ya see? The new king did not know Joseph and knew not the good things that Joseph did for Egypt. He did not trust the Hebrews, for they were too many. So the new Pharaoh made them toil and work hard, never allowing them to come together and take arms against him. The Hebrews became the Egyptians' slaves. They far outnumbered the*

Egyptians. As Ashanti is listening she begins to think; contemplating what Sam is preaching about. Her people are in bondage just like the Hebrews Sam is talking about.

Now, the Pharaoh had all the Hebrew boys killed cuz', ya see, he was worried 'bout one of them risin' up and takin' over Egypt. One of the Hebrew women did not want her new born son to die, so she made a little, bitty boat; small enough to fit a child. She let it go a float and the child ended up down the river, where the Egyptian royalty bathed. He was discovered by one of the Pharaoh's many daughters. She named the boy Moses. Moses was raised in the way of the Egyptians. After a while, Moses found out that he was a Hebrew and he stopped worshiping the Egyptians' Gods.

Sam continues reading out of the bible with more passion in his voice. *Moses looked unto Pharaoh and said, "Let my people go!" Pharaoh did not listen, so God allowed the plagues to fall upon Egypt. Finally, Pharaoh let Moses and the rest of the Hebrews go. The Hebrews left in large numbers, never wanting to return to Egypt. The Pharaoh changed his mind and sent the chariots out after Moses and the rest of the Hebrews. Moses and the rest of the Hebrew stopped at the banks of the Red Sea. The Hebrews began to get nervous and wanted to know how they were going to get across. Moses prayed holding up his stick and the Red Sea opened, allowing the Hebrews to cross. As the last few Hebrew were climbing up the bank, the Pharaoh's chariots were comin' through the path that God had opened to allow the Hebrews to cross. Moses then held up his staff, closing the Red Sea, drowning the Egyptians who followed.*

The people cheer and begin to celebrate. Sam keeps on narrating the story. *Days passed and they have not left too far from the river banks. Ya see, the people's hearts getin' nervous and impatient. Some of them even thought about goin' back to the Pharaoh, cuz' they were so desperate. Moses did not know what to do, so he began to pray. He heard the voice of God telling him to go up a nearby mountain. Moses did, and God spoke to him the Ten Commandments and wrote them into the side of a mountain called Sinai. The first commandment is: honor thy mother and father, thou shalt not kill,"* he reads all the commandments to his congregation. The preacher raises his hands and arms, which makes whoever that is sitting, to stand. An unusual breeze makes the tree sway from side to side. Sam looks at MayBell, Bulla and Geechee, who start to sing softly, 'Wade in de wadah, wade in de wadah, cheeren. The rest of the congregation starts humming as the three ladies sing.

MayBell, Geechee and Bulla start to sing a little louder and the humming gets louder as well. MayBell's, Geechee's and Bulla's voice are strong and beautiful. Ashanti begins to think about the singing that went on in her village. Everyone begins to sway to the singing, even the trees. Ashanti knows they can sing even louder, but for some reason they do not. Ashanti starts to memorize the words and she joins in as well. After the singing is over, everyone shakes each other's hand and hugs. To Ashanti, they act as if they have never met each other before. Ashanti is introduced, and she greets all the inhabitants of the plantation. They all seem to be happy to meet her.

Ashanti cannot wait to talk to Sam. She is so impressed by the way Sam has preached and read out of the Bible. Sam waits for her at the corner of the patch of woods next to the fields, just before it turns toward the barn, livery stable, Ashanti's home and the mansion. After Ashanti shakes the last person's hand she skips up to Sam and they begin to walk towards the mansion.

"Sam, I'z not know you be readin'.

"No, I cane't read, but I remember everythang my master told me when I be a litta chap."

"You not read the Bible?"

"No. I know word for word the whole book, by heart. I will teach you the words and make you a Christian, cuz' you be a heathen now."

"I not be no heathen, I be Ashanti, daughter of Mojo, the medicine man, from the village of Kisumu. "Mojo tell me there is nothing greater than me in the universe." She looks up in the sky and waves her arm as if she is showing Sam what she is greater than. "I not be no heathen. You, or no man, can tell me who I be." Something about the way Ashanti speaks to Sam makes him listen and take heed. He doesn't dare call her by another name, or belittle her again.

"Ok Baby Girl."

"And me name ain't Baby Girl; me name be Ashanti.

"Ok, Ashanti."

Ashanti walks away from Sam with her chest bowed out and her head held high.

Thadeus has not come to see Ashanti for the whole day. Bulla brings Ashanti dinner. Bulla knocks on Ashanti's door and Ashanti is sitting at the table day dreaming and looking around her home.

"The dowe be open." Yells out Ashanti then

Bulla walks in. "Here gal, dis here yo dinna. Cane't chu cook?"

"It's you, not chu." Ashanti corrects Bulla. " Chu, you' ya know what da hell I said." Can ya cook?"

"Yea, I can cook. I will cook next dinner if you'n let me."

"I don't know bout that one. You seem to take ova ery thang you do."

"No, I do it some time. Dat be yo job Bulla."

"Ok. Den, you can cook tamarra. I will see ya den." They smile at each other before Bulla's large body disappears behind the door as it shuts.

Next day MayBell is putting up clothes on the clothes line to dry. Ashanti sees her and gets dressed and goes outside to chat with her.

"Hi MayBell, How you doin' dis monin'?"

"I be just fine."

"You'n need help?"

"No, I be just fine."

Ashanti begins to help MayBell anyways by grabbing a sheet out of one of the three baskets that sit next to each other. As Ashanti takes one of the clothe pins to hang the sheet, MayBell snatches it from her. "I done told you I don't need yo help." says MayBell. Ashanti, a bit taken by what has just happened, jumps up in MayBell's face. "Na, I ain't goan let you'n hurt me. Don't you eva do dat to me again!"

MayBell is in shock at the fury of Ashanti. "Ok, Baby. I not do that no mo'." Ashanti looks deep into MayBell's eyes. "And my name not be Baby Girl my name be Ashanti."

"Ooook, Ashanti."

"I was goan help you, now, me not."

Ashanti walks towards the mansion, curious about why Thadeus did not see her the day before. As she comes through the kitchen she is stared down by Bulla. Ashanti stares back at her with a nasty stare as well.

I be trying to be friend wit' everyone, dey not want to be friend back wit' me. "I no try to be friend wit' dem no mo. I be mean and nasty to dem now.

As Ashanti leaves the kitchen, she hears talking in the game room. She recognizes one of the voices as Thadeus's and does not recognize the other. She slowly creeps to the edge of the door and peers around the corner to see whom Thadeus is talking to. It is a gentleman who is telling Thadeus, "My chest and my Belly been burning and hurting fo' the last few days." When he burps out Ashanti recognizes the smell and immediately runs into the kitchen to talk to Bulla. "Who dat be with Thadeus?" That be Thadeus's brother, he name Douglas." "You be havin' dat stuff dat make da bread rise?" Ashanti asks Bulla. MayBell nods her head yes. "Why?"

"I just need some."

MayBell points to a container on a shelf. Ashanti grabs it and pours some of its content into a glass. She looks around the kitchen and finds a few more ingredients. She goes outside to the patch of woods that's behind her house and takes some leaves off a bush. She comes back into the kitchen and puts the leaves in a cup, then puts all the ingredients in a pot, which she brings to a boil. She then pours the ingredients back into the cup that is sitting on a saucer. She slowly walks back toward the game room, careful not to spill the contents of the cup. She shyly walks into the room with her head slightly bent downward and her eyes focused on the two men. When she gets closer to Thadeus's brother she hands the cup to him.

"Well, well, well, look what we have here." initiates the man.

"Don't well, well that one, cuz' ain't nobody going to get none of that."

Ashanti looks up at Thadeus's brother and hands him the cup and saucer. "You'n drink dat and you'n be feelin'betta soon. It be hot, blow on it some," she advises. Thadeus's brother sits the cup down on a table. "I am going to let it cool down a spell and then I will drink it right down. I done heard tell a lot about you, Baby Girl. Thadeus talks about you as if he got a black angel. You're a cutie." Thadeus grabs Ashanti and puts his arm around her neck. Ashanti slightly bends her head down and bashfully smiles, turning her head into Thadeus's chest. Douglas reaches out to shake her hand. As he is shaking her hand he says. "You are smart as you are beautiful, and dat says a lot cuz' niggas are dumb as rocks." That statement did not sit well with Ashanti. A kiss on the forehead by Thadeus changes her mood.

Thadeus and his brother continue to talk until they are interrupted by Ashanti. "You not be let it get too cold cuz' it work betta when warm." insists Ashanti.

"I'm goin' to take your word for it." He walks over to the table, takes the drink and begins chugging it down. After he finishes the concoction, you can tell by the expression on his face how awful it tasted. He wipes his mouth with his sleeve. "Damn girl, what did I done drank? I hope it don't kill me." Noises start coming from his stomach. He grabs his chest, then his stomach. Those are signs that Ashanti has been anticipating. He lets out a big burp from his mouth, and a long fart, from his behind. Ashanti and Thadeus start laughing out loudly at Douglas's release of pressure. Both actions made him bend down, changing his posture.

"Well, I'll be, feel much better now. I've been hurtin' for days." He grabs Ashanti from under Thadeus's arm and begins kissing and hugging her really tight. Thadeus grabs Ashanti back from his brother because Douglas is getting too close and his kisses are beginning to get too passionate. "All right, all right, we get it. Yo drunk ass feels better now."

Douglas has the look of a dog that has just had a bone taken away from it. "I see what you been talkin about, Thadeus. You got somethin there. You damn show do." Geechee is standing at the door with Thadeus's brother's hat, anticipating him to leave. He takes the hat and swats Geechee on the butt as he walks past her. That swat on the butt makes Geechee smile a little. Geechee curtseys to Thadeus and rolls her eyes at Ashanti before leaving. Ashanti walks in front of Thadeus and crosses her arms, turning half way around saying, "You be not likin me no mo' Thadeus"

"Say more, not mo.' Ashanti looks at him and says, "Mooore."

"That's right, more. Now Baby Girl, I have to go to a special service at church today. And after service, I was invited over to a friend's house for dinner. And as you know, you can't go to these places with me."

"I be undastan'."

"I know you enjoy meeting and being around your own people." Thadeus continues, "I also know Sam did some good preachin because he was owned by a preacher before my father bought him."

"Yea, Thadeus he be good. He make me feel like I am back home. Now, I ain't goin' to church every Sunday, and the days that I don't, I can wait for you to get out of church. Why don't you be goin' to our church?"

"I don't go to colored churches, they are for your own kind."

"I thought you'n said yo God made ery body."

"I can't explain it to you cuz' that's just the way it is. I can't do nothing about it," explains Thadeus. "Enough of that church stuff, I got work to do 'round here. You can see how we run this place, by just keeping your eyes open," he concludes. Thadeus shows Ashanti around the working plantation again. As they go around it, she takes mental notes and sees a lot of flaws in the way things are being done. Ashanti immediately puts her own two cents in every aspect of what is going on. She has the dairy and beef cattle eat in different pastures. She shows Thadeus how to build irrigation ditches from the lake to the fields. She puts the crops that needed the most water closer to the lake, and the ones that create water, by themselves, further away. When her fellow workers get sick or injured, she will heal them right up and have them back working in no time. Douglas begins to tell people about how good Ashanti is at healing and word of it spreads like wild fire. People begin to call on Thadeus so he can allow Ashanti to heal them and deliver their babies. Of course, they have to pay him because he loves money. They call on him so he can allow Ashanti to heal and deliver livestock babies as well. She performs her duties very well. She is paid for her services and gives most of the money to Thadeus and keeps some for herself. Thadeus is gone on business and is not always home to know about all the money transactions. Thadeus trusts Ashanti and tells all the people she helps that it is ok to give Ashanti the money for his services. Ashanti has crops planted and they grow so fast they seem to catch up with what has already been planted.

On this evening Ashanti goes to the mansion to talk to Thadeus. "Thadeus we need to be takin our ride today.

"Now Baby Girl you know we takes that ride every Friday the day before free day."

"I know I know Thadeus but me need to speak wit ya now."

"Ok Baby Girl we will take our ride today."

Thadeus motions to one of the boys to go hitch the horse team as they stand in the door way looking towards the livery stable. As they start their ride Ashanti speaks out. "Thadeus we need a pair of dem mules cuz' the ones we be havin aint got long befo them be heading to pasture.

Thadeus looks at Ashanti with pure love and admiration in his eyes and says. "Baby Girl you neva cease to amaze me." Thadeus will do exactly what Ashanti wants him to do. He does not want to interrupt the smooth flow of the plantation that Ashanti has created.

As they ride they see another wagon coming towards them. Thadeus realizes it is old man Nate McCrae pulling two teams of mules and a saddled horse behind him. Thadeus also notices a new plow in the back of the wagon.

"What da ya say dair Ol Nate."

"Everythang is just fine and dandy this way Ol Thadeus."

"What are you gonna do with those two fine mule teams ya got there."

"Well um bringin' dem to the Baily place to sell to him." "In fact I'm selling him everythang I got wit me and ride back home on my horse."

"OL Nate I need a pair of dem mules something awful."

"Well I done promised dem to old man Baily."

"Ahhh come on Nate I need dem badly."

"Well Thadeus um o tell ya what um goan do."

"If you can get the money right now I will sell you a team."

"How much?" Thadeus replies.

Nate motions for Thadeus to lean forward and Nate whispers the price in Thadeus's ear. They both lean back into their wagons and Nate says. "I don't talk business in front of Niggras." "Dang Nate I can't get the money 'til tomorrow from the bank. I can get you the money first thing in the morning when the bank opens. If I leave now the bank will be closed by the time I get there."

"Well Thadeus that's all I can do." Ashanti leans over and whispers something in Thadeus's ear. "Tell Ol Nate to come to the house and bring the mules." Thadeus looks at Ashanti as if he did not hear what she just said. Ashanti leans back over and again whispers in his ear. "Did ya hear what me just said, tell Ol Nate to bring dem mules on to da house." "Ol Nate can't whisper cuz' I heard the price of dem mules." There is something in Ashanti's voice that makes Thadeus listen to what she has just told him. Thadeus listens and he tells Nate to come to his plantation.

When they arrive Thadeus tells Nate to park his wagon at the end of the U shaped drive way and Geechee will show him to the game room. "Nate I think I have enough 'round here to scrape up to get dem dair mules." Only reason um doing this is cuz' my daddy and old man Wellington was best of friends." "We are to Nate." "I know Thadeus, that's why I'm here. Ok Thadeus I will be waitin.'" "Can you come down some on the price?" "I can come down some but these are prized mules and I can get top dollar for them." "OK Nate"

Thadeus tells Tiny and JoJo to unhitch the mules and bring them to the livery stable. Ashanti starts walking back towards her house and Thadeus follows. Thadeus catches up with Ashanti and says. "Girl what you done did telling' me to have that man come here and you know I aint got the money on me." Even though Thadeus is verbally uneasy he is relaxed and relieved because he knows he is in good hands with his Baby Girl. They both go into Ashanti's house and Ashanti motions for Thadeus to sit at her kitchen table. She looks behind her bed and grabs one of two churns that she has hidden. It is very heavy but she manages to bring it to the kitchen table. Ashanti tips over the churn allowing its contents to spill on to the table. It is a whole lot of pennies dimes nickels and quarters. Thadeus's eyes pop open at what he is witnessing. She smiles as she bends down and looks into Thadeus's eyes and says. "Ya got to save fo a rainy day." Thadeus instantly envisions in his mind the day he gave and taught Ashanti about money. Thadeus jumps up out of his seat to embrace Ashanti and she begins to run from him. He catches up to her, turns her towards him and begins squeezing and kissing her all over her face and says, "God has blessed me with you. My God are you good." Thadeus swats her on her butt shaking his head. Ashanti looks back at him with a smile on her face glowing from what he just said.

They both sit down and start counting the money. They only use a third of what Ashanti has saved. "By the way where did you get all this money?" Before Ashanti could answer Thadeus says, "No no don't tell me I don't need to know." "Now Thadeus forget that I got this money, It only be here fo' impotent thangs." Thadeus grabs Ashanti and pulls her in his arms and says." The word is important and say things not thangs." Ashanti repeats after him as they are both gathering the money to give to Ol Nate. Before they get to the door Ashanti stops and says to Thadeus. "I want you to remember this. There is more in taking care of the money den makin' it." He winks and kisses Ashanti on the cheek and says. "Ok Baby Girl." They bring the change and bills to Nate who says. "Y'all dam show did have to scrape the bottom of the barrel to get this money." I'm going to use the dollar bills and keep savin this change fo a rainy day." Ashanti boldly speaks out before Nate can finish his sentence. "cuz' there is more in takin' care of then makin' it" The phrase that came out of Ashanti's mouth stuns Nate. He began picking his brain on where he heard that phrase before, and then he bursts out. "My mama use to say something like that." He smiles at Ashanti, shakes Thadeus's hand and climbs up on his wagon tipping his hat as he leaves. Thadeus yells out to Nate. "What you gonna tell old man Baily." "Don't worry Thadeus we are all set." Ashanti starts thinking. "I'm glad I put most of the dollar bills, silver, and gold dollars in the other churn." "cuz' you can't always let your left hand know what your right hand is doing."

The next day while Thadeus is at a social affair, the town veterinarian shows up and wants to talk to him. He sees Thadeus and walks towards him while he is speaking to other gentlemen. The gentlemen are dressed neatly with their high top hats and tails; watching as the other men twirls their women about as they dance. "Hey Thadeus, how's it going?" shouts the doctor as he tries to talk over the music.

"I'm doing fine doc, how are you?"

"I am doing fine. Seems like I got more time since that gal of yours been around." states the doctor. Thadeus doesn't know whether to smile or to give a look of concern for what the veterinarian has just said. "Well doc, it seems like you needed a little help around here, so I have my Baby Girl help people you can't get to."

"Oh no Thadeus, I'm not mad at all. I could not get to all the people. I was working day and night; did not know if I was coming or going. Now I got time to go down to the creek and do some fly fishing, a little hunting and spend more time with my grand chaps. If anything, I want to thank her and you for giving me some time for myself. I would like to meet her. I have a few questions I would like to ask her about some of her healing methods for humans and animals," confesses the doctor. Not only does the vet cure animals, he also heals and sees after humans. Thadeus is happy with what he just heard. He swings his cup from left to right keeping up with the beat of the music.

Thadeus's livestock is multiplying like magic. Every time Sam looks around he hears another baby animal calling its mother. One morning Thadeus comes to the livery stable to get the buggy and horses Sam is hitching up. Ashanti sees Thadeus and comes out of her house to surprise him. She stops just before she gets to the door waiting to scare him when he pulls out with the team of horses. While she is standing there she can hear everything that's being said.

"Thadeus, I don't quite know what to say."

"What do you mean Sam?"

"There are animals coming out of nowhere. I ain't neva seen anything like this befo. My granny use to tell us about some bad and evil magic that go on back there in Africa."

"Listen Sam." interrupts Thadeus. "Having more animals is making our plantation bigger and me, rich. I don't see that as being a problem."

"Well, you can feel that way if you'n wanna, but I don't trust it."

"Well, you keep an eye on it and tell me if you see some of that Hoodoo, Mojo stuff going on."

Ashanti is surprised at what she has just heard. *Sam must be telling Thadeus I am bad, and maybe some of his people are from villages around where I was born; cuz', how Thadeus know about Mojo and Hoodoo, talking about them that way? I'm goin' to look out for Sam, as he is watching me. I will show Thadeus, I ain't goan let nothing hurt him or this here place we's got.*

Thadeus smiles and hops into the carriage. With a flick of his wrist the team of horses takes off.

Ashanti happily skips to the slave quarters to see what is going on. It's toward the end of the hot summer and the inhabitants of the plantation seem to be really up beat and happy to go to work this morning. Ashanti is up every morning like she has been doing for most of the mornings as the summer passes by. She asks one of her fellow coworkers, "What's going on, why's everyone so happy?" The coworker responds as he skips towards the field, "It be time to lay it by."

"What is that?" inquires Ashanti.

"Dat mean, after we finish, we ain't got nuttin' to do but pickin' the crop and bring it to the market." *How someone could be so happy to work for free? These white folks must be worshipin' Gaunab to have put roots on all my people. That's why white folks don't wanna go to church with us. The God out dat book we be prayin' to must not be as strong as their God, cuz' my people still in bondage. Sam talk about Pharaoh and how them Hebrews got free, what about us? I guess Gaunab be the one that runs things around here. How white folks know about Gaunab?"*

Chapter VIII

Great Day! Thadeus is very happy that Ashanti has come. He seems to have more money than he can spend. He does not get in his work clothes anymore because Ashanti runs and takes care of everything. He now dresses like a gentleman every day. He is always prospecting new business ventures and is constantly thinking about how he can make more money. He sleeps with Ashanti on most nights, but there are many nights in which he doesn't come home at all. He goes up north, to see where he can sell his crops and invest his money.

Coming home after one such visit to the north he brings Ashanti a gift. He opens the door and Ashanti is already in her bed. She yells out, "Thadeus!" and runs and jumps into Thadeus's arms, almost knocking him to the floor.

"Come on Baby Girl, are you trying to kill me?"

"No, no, Thadeus, you just be gone too long and I missed you so."

"I got something for you." He says this while he dangles a box behind him. He pushes her back with one arm as she reaches for the box. He finally hands it to her and she starts ripping it open as fast as she can. She pulls the contents out and asks, "What's this?"

"It's what they call a negligee." "It's from Paris, France. It's the latest thing that all the women are wearing. Go in the bedroom and put it on so I can have a peek." Ashanti puts it on and comes slinking out her bed room. She has a body that makes the negligee look like a master piece. She turns around, displaying all her curves, stopping in front of Thadeus with her hands on her hips. Thadeus ushers Ashanti back into her bedroom, lays her on her bed and begins to make love to her.

Next morning Thadeus is awakened by the roosters and Ashanti, who has her face in her hands, and her elbows holding her face and hands up. "Thadeus, what good is you buying that for me, when you take it right off me in the blink of an eye?" Thadeus starts laughing, grabbing Ashanti as he rolls her on top of him, at the same time rolling on his back. He looks into her big round eyes and just smiles. Thadeus gets up and heads for the mansion after he kisses Ashanti on the forehead, telling her that he has to go help his brother get his plantation running. Not long after Thadeus leaves, Ashanti gets up and gets dressed and heads over to the livery stable where she sees Sam working. Sam is pumping the bellows to make the coals hot so he can beat and fix a horse shoe. Ashanti stands in front of Sam.

"Sam, I be wontin' to know a little bit more 'bout Moses and the slaves that were set free to leave Egypt."

"What do you wanna know?"

"If dey God set dem free, why cane't he let us be free?"

The words that come out of Ashanti's mouth just stopped Sam right in his tracks. He puts the horse shoe and the tools that he's been using to hold the red hot horse shoe down. He says, "Shhhhhh!" He walks to the door of the livery stable and looks both ways before he walks back to Ashanti and says, "Girl, I mean Ashanti, you cane't be talkin' 'bout that kinda stuff 'round here. We will get whipped to death for talkin' 'bout stuff like that. When I know for a fact that nobody be about, I tell you all you wanna know. Now, goan scat," he says this as he is shooing her like a bunch of chickens that have wandered in the wrong place. Ashanti reluctantly walks out of the livery stable without her question having been answered. As she walks away she begins humming "Wade in the water, wade in the water, children."

Before she reaches the slave quarters she hears something in the woods. She stops and peers into the section of woods where the noise is coming from. When the object comes into focus she realizes that it is Dingo. He waves his arm motioning for Ashanti to come to him. She slowly walks to him and he takes her hand, leading her further into the woods. He stops and turns around, looking into her big brown eyes.

"Ashanti, I been thinkin' 'bout you e'ry day. I want you to be me own."

"Thadeus not like dat"

"Me not care 'bout that! Me take chance ta have ya."

"Thadeus will kill you if he finds out."

"I not care. I be wontin' you since I see ya."

"Dingo, I think you be a fine man, but I not do dat to Thadeus. He be da only man dat go up in me."

Dingo puts Ashanti's hand into his pants. Ashanti grips what he has and pulls it out. Ashanti's eyes pop wide open at what she has in her hand. "Na, do masta have dis?! No, no, Dingo; Thadeus ain't got dis. Ya need to go inta the barn or the stable to find one of deese. I cane't let you put dat in me. Thadeus be knowin' somethin' not be right wit' his stuff." She is walking backwards as she says this; while Dingo is still standing in front of her with his manhood hanging almost to his knee; as if he is trying to make Ashanti change her mind and put it inside her.

"Ok Dingo, I be seein' you 'round. That be Geechee's stuff anyway."

For some reason Dingo takes off running. Ashanti, not knowing why Dingo took off, turns around and finds out what has spooked him. It is Geechee, who is coming for reasons unknown. The only time she comes this way is when she goes to church on God's day or to get Dingoed. Ashanti immediately thinks of a way to mess with Geechee's mind. Ashanti comes out of the woods with a semi limp. She continues to limp until she stops to meet Geechee.

"Girl, what chu doin' comin' out dose woods yonder, and why you be limpin' so?"

"Why you be askin all deese questions. I do not have to tell you nuthin'."

Geechee quickly takes off past Ashanti heading into the woods where she has had many rendezvous with Dingo. Geechee gets to the slave quarters and asks. "Where be Dingo." An old lady sitting on the porch snapping green beans points to the north field. Geechee walks over there as fast as she can, with the thought of her man messing with Ashanti. She arrives at the edge of the field and waves to Dingo to come to her. He is hoeing around cotton plants, ridding them of weeds. When Dingo reaches Geechee he takes her in his big strong arms.

"Hi Geechee," he greets her. She pulls away from him, loosening his strong grip, like she is the one who has the power. "You done did Baby Girl, didn't you!" "What you be talkin' bout? I be out here workin'."

"I see she comin' out da woods where you be meetin' me at. Pull it out so I'z can smell it!"

"Girl, you done lost yo mind!" replies Dingo in an incredulous tone as he turns around and starts walking back into the field.

"If 'ns you'n did her you not be gettin' no mo of dis."

As she speaks she pats her pubic mound displaying what he is not going to get anymore. He turns around as she is leaving and says, "You be knowin' me, if me a goan up in her she would not be walkin' right!" That infuriates Geechee even more as she storms back toward Ashanti's house.

Geechee gets to Ashanti's house and barges through the door. "Now, you listen, Baby Girl, ya betta stay way from my man! Ya already got Thadeus, so ya betta stay way from Dingo!" As she says this she is chest to chest with Ashante backing her up against the wall. Ashanti, a little overwhelmed and shocked by Geechee's actions and aggression which puts her in a daze that she quickly snaps out of. As Ashanti begins to speak, she reverses the momentum held by Geechee as she pushes her in the opposite direction. "Na, listen, you need to be knockin' befo' you'n, I mean you come in! And my name be Ashanti not no dam Baby Girl!"

Geechee, who has stopped in her tracks replies, "Like I said Baby Girl."

"Don't you worry 'bout who's gettin' this, you better worry 'bout yo own stuff, not mine!" says Ashanti as she nudges Geechee past the threshold and slams the door in her face. Geechee, really upset, storms down the steps toward the mansion. Ashanti sits in one of the chairs around her table and starts laughing at the event that just took place.

Geechee arrives back at the mansion and enters through the back where she sees MayBell and Bulla standing in the kitchen talking. "Dat little bitch Baby Girl is at Dingo," claims Geechee. "Ain't she got enough?" Bulla turns around and faces Geechee. "You know Thadeus breeds Dingo all ova da county. Hell he done breed him with both of us fo' you came 'round." MayBell puts her two cents in. "He'n stick anythang 'round here. He'n poke a snake if you hold he head." MayBell and Bulla start laughing. You can tell by Geechee's expression that she does not think this is funny. "I'z really do not think Ashanti wont anythang wit no Dingo," says Bulla. "She be too smart fo' dat. She be just messin' wit' chow head, Geechee." Geechee starts thinking about how she is going to get rid of Ashanti. Ashanti has gotten Geechee's closest friends to laugh at her.

"I got a right mind to tell Thadeus dat Ashanti been doin' it wit Dingo." says Geechee. Bulla turns around as she walks out of the room. "Na, you'n bet not get no idea 'bout tellin Thadeus, cuz' if you'n ain't right, it will be hell ta pay."

Geechee begins to think, "Just wait, she soon make a mistake, and me goan ruin she life."

Chapter IX

The evening comes and Thadeus walks in through the front door. He yells out.

"Hey, hey! Daddy's home, where everyone be?"

Geechee, MayBell and Bulla rush to come and greet him, Thadeus smiles, looking, waiting and anticipating to be greeted by someone special.

Geechee speaks, "Thadeus, we need to go to town soon cuz' we be needin' a lot of thangs fo' da house."

"Well, just make a list of the things that we need and you and Baby Girl can go to town and get them." Geechee is enraged by what she just heard. "Baby Girl cane't read; I cane't read." replies Geechee. "Well, you and her better come up with something cuz' that chore ain't mine's no mo', I mean, more. Ashanti is smart, she will come up with something to make sure y'all get everything," assures Thadeus. Geechee is not happy; Ashanti has come between her and Thadeus again. Geechee does not share, nor does anything with Thadeus any more since Ashanti's arrival.

The next morning Sam, Ashanti and Geechee are off to town to pick up goods the mansion and the plantation needs. What they call town is the center where government and commerce is held. It is in the center of BrookHaven. Sam is driving, and Ashanti is sitting in the middle of Sam and Geechee. Ashanti breaks the silence, "Sam, now you can talk about what us was goan talk about." Sam hits Ashanti with the side of his knee, while pointing at Geechee with his eyes. Geechee is leaning and looking in the other direction, not wanting to talk or look at Ashanti. He shakes his head no, which makes Ashanti realize that this is not a conversation to be discussed in front of Geechee.

"What be the town, Sam?"

"Well, Miss Ashanti, that be where we go shopping for things we don't make back home. It's a wonderful place where there is a lot of people walkin' 'round, handlin' they business. You are goin' to love the excitement of where we are goin'." Ashanti squirms a little in her seat anticipating what she is going to witness.

As they come around a corner, the change of scenery explodes. There are buildings on both sides of the street with big signs on them. People are walking around, both Africans and whites. Some of the blacks are accompanied by their owners and some are taking care of business on their own. There are beautiful dresses in some of the windows. There is even a building with a big tooth on it. Sam yells out, "Wooooo!" as he pulls back on the reins to stop the horses. He pulls in front of a building that has cloth, shovels, and picks in a big window. Sam slides down off the wagon slowly, allowing his old body to easily touch the ground. He walks around the other side of the wagon and assists Geechee and then Ashanti, off the wagon.

Ashanti tells us her experience that day: *I continued looking around, seeing the new sights. I even tripped over the front steps looking. Then I walked up the stairs and into the front door, where there were pretty clothes and everything that the plantation needs. I stopped in my tracks when I saw the large glass jars full of objects with all the colors of the rainbow in them. My eyes were attached to colors that mesmerized me.*

The owner sees that Ashanti looks almost as if she is under a spell, just by looking at the candy. He reaches into one of the jars, grabbing one of the candies. Looking at Sam, he asks, "Hey Sam, what's her name?" Taking his hat and humbly bending down Sam answers, "Sir, her name be Baby." Ashanti immediately looks at Sam with a hard look, "Ah ah ah, her name be Ashanti."

"Ok Ashanti, Here take this," offers the owner of the store. Ashanti slowly lifts her hand and takes the candy bashfully, thanking the store's owner, while displaying her pretty white teeth and dimples that accent her smile. Ashanti unwraps the rainbow colored candy and puts it in her mouth. *"Wow, this is so good. This is what a rainbow must taste like. I wonder where he got this from. These white people must be worshiping Gaunab. They just must be."*

The man looks at Ashanti, "I heard tell a lot about you from your master and his brother. I think they're right. I sense something special about you. And any nigga that makes a whole heap of money for their master is a good nigga." Ashanti forgets about how good the candy tastes as she listens to what the man has just told her. She smiles and plays it off, not letting the man know that she is not pleased with what he just said. They gather up the provisions the man has put on the counter and start loading them on the wagon. A tall, brown skinned, well-built man also helps them load the wagon. He must be owned by the store's owner. He smiles at Ashanti so much that it starts to make Ashanti uncomfortable. He looks at Ashanti the same way Ashanti was looking at the candy in the jar. Geechee sees what is going on and walks by displaying her goods, which provokes the man to stare and smile. Then he looks back at Ashanti, showing her that she was the new and improved object of his desire. When Geechee turns to give the man a sexy glance, she finds his eyes are fixed back on Ashanti, which makes Geechee very upset. Once again, if looks could kill, Ashanti would be a dead woman.

When they are done loading the wagon, Sam slowly climbs back up to his seat in the same manner he came down, slow and easy. Geechee quickly runs past Ashanti so that the big brown skinned man can help her up on the wagon before Ashanti. Geechee gives him a sexy look as he helps her up onto the wagon. Geechee's sexy glance immediately disappears when he reaches his hand out to Ashanti, grabbing under her arm pit and her thigh, as he assists Ashanti up. "What yo name be?" asks the man.

"Now, Albert, you know what my name be?"

"I know dat Geechee, um talkin' bout de fine young tenda here."

Ashanti smiles while batting her long thick eyelashes. "My name be Ashanti," He reaches for her hand and Ashanti gives it to him and he kisses it, just in time before Sam pops the reins and they take off.

Geechee is boiling mad because Ashanti has stolen all her glory. They ride in the opposite direction from the way they came. As they head down the street Geechee happens to see Mr. Gilbert Poole working at his feed shop. She smiles with the menacing look of a hyena, ready to eat leftovers from a lion's kill. Meanwhile, Ashanti begins to notice signs and landmarks that she has seen before. She yells out, "That be the barn where they keep us at after we got off the big canoe." They keep traveling until they reach the place where a lot of people are gathered. Ashanti sees where she was auctioned off. Her heart grows heavy as she passes the spot where the man with the fast mouth is talking and a black woman is standing on the same spot where she stood. They catch each other's eyes, and she can feel the same despair that she once felt, in the young woman's eyes. This makes Ashanti's heart heavy with grief. She knows how the girl standing on the platform being auctioned off feels. *Why do people do such terrible things? Being taken from somewhere they love and had a future. It just don't make no sense at all.* She also thinks about Mojo and the village, and how one day she was going to become the medicine woman of her village.

They arrive back home and there are men waiting to unload the wagon. Sam brings himself down and walks to the other side while waiting for Ashanti because they are going in the same direction. Geechee hops down off the wagon with a silly smile and silly look on her face. She skips up the sidewalk as if she was a happy little girl. Sam and Ashanti start walking toward her house and the livery stable. "Ashanti, I did not want to talk in front of Geechee, she may tell Thadeus." "Ya see, in this country there are places where black folks be free. I was told to follow the North Star, it will take you to freedom."

"Well Sam, I be in love wit' Thadeus, I not wanna leave him."

"Well Miss Ashanti, you goan have to choose between him or yo freedom. Ashanti, here come Thadeus, we goan have to talk 'bout dis 'notha time." Thadeus greets them, "Hey, y'all take care of business in town?"

"Yea, we got everything we need," replies Ashanti as she hugs him.

"I knew everything would be all right because you were there," says Thadeus with a confident tone of voice. "What I did was to have Sam, me and Geechee each have our own things to get, dat made it easy."

"Not dat, say that." says Thadeus as he corrects Ashanti's pronunciation.

"That," says Ashanti.

"Ok, that was a good idea. I knew it would work out just fine."

Thadeus loosens himself from Ashanti's hold and heads back toward the mansion.

"Where you be goin' Thadeus?"

"I got some business to take care of. You got a surprise at your house when you get there."

Ashanti leaves Thadeus. She starts running home to see what her surprise is. For some reason, Sam is hurrying to get home as well.

When Ashanti gets home, there is a whole lot of chaps sitting on her porch and playing in front of her house. They all greet her. She is happy to see them, as they all come and hug her. One of the lantern holders says, "You be from Africa and you be knowin' night stories from dair." Ashanti is curious about how they seem to know so much about her. One of the lantern boys walks into the house and gets a chair out and puts it on the porch. She sits down and begins to tell the children about her Gods. She starts by saying. *Now, what I'm about to tell y'all, y'all cane't be tellin' nobody cuz' they will stop me from tellin' y'all anything. Every time it be thunderin' and lightin', that be shangó letting us know he be 'round these parts, for us to be still and listen.* The children continue to listen to her until the calling of their mothers break their concentration from listening to Ashanti tell her stories. They all say at the same time, "When will ya tell us mo'?"

"Now, don't y'all fret none, I ain't goan nowhere," says Ashanti as she pats the heads of a few of them before they leave. She stops them. "Like I always tell y'all, you do good things, and good things will come to ya. Y'all do bad things, and Gaunab goan get y'all," she scowls and bares her teeth. "rrraaaaaah!" the children take off running.

Ashanti continues to heal people and animals alike. She also directs her fellow captives and pretty much handles the business of the plantation. She wants to take part in her first harvest of cotton; she wants to learn every aspect of the process. She also continues to talk about Africa and all the stories she contains. The livestock are multiplying so much that Thadeus can afford to give some of them to his brother, and still make a major profit. Ashanti's healing and medicine also puts money in Thadeus's pocket. Now Thadeus doesn't sleep with Ashanti as much as he used to. They are both now very busy and neither of them have noticed the trend in which they have fallen in. Ashanti has also learned how to ride the wagon into town, which has enabled her to take care of business without Sam. The horses practically dance when Ashanti is behind the straps controlling them.

One day, she is going to town with both of the lamp holders. "Y'all ain't told me y'alls names" says Ashanti. "I know y'all name cane't be 'lamp boys'." They both chuckle, "Naw, that not be our name," answers one of them. "My name be Tiny." He is the bigger of the two, with brown, reddish hair on his round head. He has thick lips with very white teeth. He is going to be a handsome young man when he grows up. He favors Dingo a little.

"Who yo parents be?" requests Ashanti. Tiny sits straight, bowing up his chest. "My daddy name be Dingo and my mama be MayBell."

"Now that I look at you, you show do look like both of dem." The other boy clears his throat, as if he needs to be specially introduced. "Uuum, excuse me, my name be Joseph, but ery body call me 'Nuff' or JoJo."

"Why they call you dat?"

"I show nuff can get anythang done."

"Half ass," says Tiny as he shoves Joseph. Joseph has a light brown complexion and curly hair. It is evident that he gets lighter during the winter because on the underside of his arm he is lighter, as if the sun has tanned only one side of his arm. He will also be a handsome man when he grows older.

"Now, who do yo mama be?"

"My daddy be Thadeus and my mama be Bulla," says Joseph.

"Oh, I see, yo mamas be together, so y'all be together" says Ashanti in an affirming tone. Tiny looks at Ashanti sideways and says, "Sumtin' like dat."

"How old y'all be?"

"We both be fourteen. We be two months apart." Ashanti is only a few years older than them in age, but she's many years ahead of them in maturity.

"Why don't y'all be wit' the uda chaps when they come sit on my porch when I be tellin' dem 'bout our home land?"

"Ain't my homeland. Dis be where I from," replies Tiny. Joseph says, "I know dat where we come from, don't mind him, he can sometimes be an ignant nigga. I came one time don't you remember? Well anyways, if you got sumtin' to tell us, we be listenin', We be all da time havin' sumtin' ta do e'ry day, dat's why we don't get dair to sit a spell witcha like we would like to." Tiny nudges Joseph in the ribs. "Ok boy, dis boy wonna know how old you be." As Joseph is talking, Tiny turns around bashfully, twirling his pointed toes on the floor of the wagon. Ashanti reaches past Joseph and softly pinches Tiny on his cheek. "I be almost nineteen, and I be Thadeus's and I be a litta too old fo y'all." "K nuff of dat," Joseph replies. "Please Ms. Ashanti, do tell, we be wontin' to know 'bout Africa."

"Well, there was a spida named Anansi," "She had the wisdom and the intelligence of a person dat has been on the earth for a long time. Ya see, she be havin' her own place wit' a large mud wall dat be all 'round her house. She be gettin' some chickens soon and she need somebody to watch dem at night cuz' lots of animals will kill and eat dem.

One day, Osebo de leopard came out of de woods and he be walkin' by Anansi's house. Anansi says, 'Hey, Osebo, will you see afta my chickens at night?' Osebo be smilin' from ear to ear. 'Ok Anansi, I goan be de one to watch over yo chickens.' As Osebo was speaking, Aneyha de hyena stepped out de same patch of bushes Osebo did. 'Anansi, you know he be de one dat eat all de chickens? Me be de one dat watch dem for ya, says Aneyha. Ok Aneyha, I be de one dat give a piece of steak e'ry morning fo watchin' me chickens.' Osebo walked off looking back at Anansi as he disappeared into the bushes. Before he was out of sight he yell to Anansi, 'You be knowin'me fer a long time, you know I won't lie. You don't even know him like dat. Don't listen to Osebo. He don't know what he be talkin' bout.' The chickens are dropped off and Anansi puts them in the coop."

"Night falls and the Aneyha watches the coup from behind the tall wall that surrounds Anansi's home. He is awakened by the crowing of one of her roosters. She gets up and goes outside to let her chickens out to feed. She counted them and they were all there. 'Brother Aneyha, here be yo piece of meat.' Anansi throws the piece of meat to the ground and Aneyha quickly gobbles it up. The next night the same thing happens. Aneyha told Anansi he did not see or hear anything. So Anansi let the chickens out and counted them and they were all there, so she gave Aneyha his piece of meat. The leopard comes back out of the bushes.

"Hey Aneyha, all you gettin' for being up all night is a piece of meat; you should be gettin' mo' food fo'dat."

"Yeah Osebo, I know me should be gettin' mo', but um o wait a while befo I ask fo' mo'.

'Ok, na 'member what I done told ya.'

"On the seventh morning Aneyha said, after gobbling up the piece of meat, 'I need mo' food, dis not 'nough."

"Well, Aneyha, we made a deal and I am keeping up with my bargain and you have to keep up with yo'ns. Mind you Aneyha, it is the dry season and fresh meat is scarce.' Anansi goes back inside her house to start her day. On this night the moon is full when Osebo the leopard comes out of the bushes again. "Man, you're still settlin' for that dinky piece of meat. You could be out dair gettin' much mo' meat den you be gettin' here. If I was you, I be ova dat wall and get me one of dem chickens." Aneyha agreed with Osebo. "I goan get one dem chickens ta night and da piece of meat in da monin.' Osebo turns away from Aneyha and starts smiling as soon as his face was out of the view of Aneyha. Osebo tries to speak but he could not until he stopped laughing. Then he yells out of the bushes, 'Aneyha, you're worth more den one piece *of meat!'*

The next morning Anansi went to the chicken coop and opened the door. She counted her chickens and one was missing. She recounted again and again. She cast a web on top of the chicken coup and pulled herself up, then climbed over the ledge and stood on top of the roof. She carefully canvased the area surrounding the chicken coup. She noticed that there were claw marks on the wall. She repelled down her web and got the meat for Aneyha to eat. Before she threw the meat over the wall to Aneyha, she asks, "Did you hear anything last night?"

"Oh no Anansi, me not hear nuttin.'

"Ok Aneyha, see you in the monin.'

For the next two nights the same thing happens again and again. Anansi had a trick up her sleeve. She stood on top of the wall waving the piece of meat around as if she could not get it off one of her many hands. Aneyha looked at Anansi with drool coming out of his mouth anticipating Anansi dropping the meat. He runs and jumps up on the wall snatchin the meat and nipping a piece of meat off Anansi's hand, leaving the same claw marks as the one in the backyard behind the chicken coop.

"I be knowin' dat it be you in da chicken coop. These are same marks that are on top of the wall in the back by the chicken coop. Be gone befo I call on Shangó to struck ya down with a lightnin' bolt!'

The Aneyha took off, wandering for days looking for some game to eat. His search was to no avail. He decides to go back to Anansi's house and ask her if he could get his job back. As soon as he walks out the bush he sees Anansi throwing a piece of meat over the wall to Osebo. He puts his head down and disappears back into the bushes."

Ashanti asks the boys, "What have you learned from this story?"

"Always be happy wit' what you got," replies Tiny.

"If somebody's feedin'ya, don't bite dey hand," says Joseph.

"You're both right," affirms Ashanti, "never bite the hand dat feeds ya, and meat in the hand is worth mo' dan a leopard in the bush. I'm happy dat you liked our story from our homeland," says Ashanti as she smiles at the two young men that are accompanying her. She has slowed down while she was telling the story, she quickly slaps the behind of both horses and they take off.

Ashanti continues her journey into town to pick up provisions for the plantation. When she pulls in front of the store she notices people looking at her and a few of them are coming in her direction. Ashanti and her two escorts go up the stairs and into the store. Tiny and Show 'Nuff immediately go to the back of the store where there are toys and balls to play with.

"I stand in front of the shelves that contain canned goods when suddenly I hear the front door open and I hear the shuffling of footsteps."

"Um, Baby Girl, my foot is swollen from dropping a log on it."

"Mr. McCarthy, fill a bucket full of hot water, make show it be where you'n can take da heat. Then put some viniga' and salt in da water. Then keep yo foot in fo' one hour, two times a day. You should be fine afta dat."

"Thanks ya kindly, Baby Girl."

This time it is a female's voice speaking, "Baby Girl, my stomach's been hurtin' for the last three days. I've been burping something that smells so bad, I cane't even take the smell."

"Make you some Onion tea."

"What's an Onion tea?"

"Well Mrs. Green, I want you ta get a frying pan and full it wit' about dis much of water," Ashanti uses her pointing finger and her thumb to show Mrs. Green the amount of water to be put in the pan. "Den take a onion and cut it up in da pan. Powe some sugar on da onions."

"How much sugar?"

" 'Bout a cup. Den, let de water come to a boil, den let it cool down. Den you drink it all up and you'n be just fine."

"Thank ya Baby Girl, thank ya."

Ashanti eyes are fixed on the canned goods on the shelves, never turning around to see who she is talking to. It is as if she has eyes in the back of her head.

The door opens again and the Bell above the door signifies it. *I hear a baby crying and a young girl walks over to me with the crying baby in her arms. She taps me on the shoulder and I turn around and see a young girl with a baby.*

"What the matta wit' yo chap?"

"Well, Ms. Baby Girl, people be tellin' me outside dat you be in here and they say dat you can help."

Ashanti takes the baby from the girl and lays it on the counter. *I rub the baby from the Belly button up towards it's throat. I then pick up the baby, turning it toward me with its face lying on my shoulder and I begin patting it on the back. The baby burps and farts at the same time. I take the baby off my shoulder and I look into her relieved eyes.*

"What she name be?"

"Her name be Ann Elizabeth."

Ashanti begins talking to the baby. "What da matta wit' my baby? They just don't know how to make auntie's baby feel betta." The baby looks at Ashanti and begins to laugh and coo. The young mother's face is relieved as Ashanti hands the baby back to her.

"How old she be?"

"She be nine months old."

"You give her tit?"

"Yea, and she tries to eat e'ry thang me and my husband eat."

"Well, don't be lettin' she eat too much our food 'till she be one," recommends Ashanti.

"Thank you Ms. Baby Girl." As the young mother is thanking Ashanti she slightly bows as she leaves, giving Ashanti the utmost respect. The mother is not a plantation owner, this is evident since she is dressed rather shabbily and her english is not much better than Ashanti's.

Ashanti and the boys gather their provisions which are on the counter. She looks towards the back and motions for the boys to come and help her put the provisions in the back of the wagon. As they come towards her, the big brown skinned man is with the boys, smiling at Ashanti from ear to ear. "I'z gonna help ya too," exclaims the man. They all grab the provisions and put them in the back of the wagon. Every time the brown skinned man has a chance he will smile in Ashanti's face. Joseph and Tiny do not like this at all as they snatch whatever the man is carrying out of his hand and put it on the back of the wagon. Tiny stops in front of the man while looking dead into his eyes. "Listen!" starts Tiny. "This is Thadeus Wellington's woman. You bess back off, fo', we tell him you be tryin' to get he stuff." The expression on the man's face immediately changes as he cowers to Tiny words: "I'z just be tryin' to help ya's. I not wont to start no trubah, I go on 'bout my business. Y'all have a good day." He turns around and quickly runs back up the steps and back into the building. Ashanti and the boys all laugh at the sight of a grown man getting shook up by the words from a young boy's mouth. They laugh their way into the wagon and down the main thruway of the town. "Everytime I come here he be smiling in my face."

Joseph and Tiny make jokes about how each one of them get hurt or messed up during work or play. Tiny seems to be the butt of all the calamities that take place. Joseph giggles, "Tiny, you 'member the time we be playin catch and I threw de ball too hard and it landed in de bushes. Tiny pushes Joseph because he doesn't want him to bring up that miserable event as Joseph laughs. "Ashanti," he continues, "The ball goan down in da bushes and knocked down a bee's nest. Tiny and me did not see da bees till Tiny come divin' out de bushes, shakin' an' dancin' cuz' da bees be turrin' he butt up." Tiny just sits there thinking about that dreadful day while Joseph and Ashanti laugh their butts off. "Nuffa dat Joseph, you be not forgettin' nuttin'." As they near the auction stand after passing the barn, they notice that no one was there, which gives Ashanti an empty feeling inside. The two boys seem to catch Ashanti's vibe because they don't say a word until they are past the terrible landmark.

When they arrive home Ashanti pulls up on the side of the mansion and Geechee, Bulla and MayBell come out to unload the provisions. Ashanti and Dingo take the wagon down by the livery stable to unload the rest. Geechee gets really upset at Ashanti and Dingo for ridding together. She goes to bed thinking about, the day in which she can hurt Ashanti badly.

Sam comes out of the door of the livery stable with a nasty look on his face. "Ashanti, why you be tellin' dese young chaps 'bout dat hoodoo voodoo shit?" "I be hearin' dem talkin' 'bout gwanna goan get ya. God don't like dat puttin' other Gods befo' he.'"

"Well, yo' God got you workin' 'round here fo' nothin.' You ain't even a man," she continues. "You tellin' dem chaps 'bout not sayin' gaunab. Is dat who you be prayin' to, an' not know it? An' I will tell dem chaps 'bout stories of dey homeland, cuz' what you'n be tellin' dem chaps is dat it be right to be a slave." Sam reacts immediately. He knows not to upset Ashanti because he wants to get rid of her. "Ashanti, you right. Dem chaps need to know and understand where dey be comin' from. And you right Ashanti." Sam comes closer to Ashanti while Dingo goes to the back of the wagon to finish unloading it. "Yeah, we need to be talkin' 'bout runnin' north to be free," continues Sam. He gets close to Ashanti, whispering in her ear, not wanting Dingo to hear what they are talking about. "I will talk to you lata 'bout dis. Ok Ashanti?" Ashanti nods her head yes as if she agrees with Sam.

She walks away thinking about what Sam has just said. *I don't trust him;*

he's too happy being a slave. I will watch out for him, to see what he's going to do in regards to us being free. But I really love Thadeus; I will just have to see and listen to what my heart tells me." Ashanti goes into her home still thinking about what Sam said and she realizes that Thadeus has not spent the night with her in a long time. *I know I been busy, as well as Thadeus, which is why we have not spent time together. I hope he realizes the same thing and come and stay with me tonight."* Ashanti is resting her head on her arms at the table. Thadeus opens the door and walks into the house putting his arm around Ashanti's neck and Ashanti instantly knows who is behind her. She grabs his arms and pulls them closer and tighter around her neck hugging him back.

"Baby Girl, you miss me?"

"I be just thinkin bout you."

Thadeus points his hand over her mouth to correct her grammar. "Not, 'I be thinkin', It's 'I am thinking'. Say I am thinking.'"

"Ok Thadeus, I am thinking 'bout how we both so busy and not have time fo' each other."

"I was thinking the same thing. I have to leave town and I will be back Friday." Ashanti stands up and turns around pouting. Thadeus grabs her chin with his index finger curled inward, "Baby Girl, I'll be back Friday and I will stay with you for the whole weekend. I promise I will not leave your sight. And I know you will hold down the fort while I'm gone."

"You don't have to say that cuz' you know I will." You gonna have to go back to town on Monday cuz' we're going to have a dance on Saturday"

"You mean, free day?"

"Like I said, Saturday."

"I know I'm goin' to be a maid like Geechee, cuz' we people cane't be moseying up wit'white peepa's."

"Damn girl, you always one step ahead of me."

"Yea, yea. Do not eva' forget dat."

"What you mean by that?"

She grabs Thadeus' arm and pulls him toward her bedroom. "Come in here and I'll show you what I mean." They go in the room and make love. After the intense love making session Thadeus gets up and Ashanti gets dressed. He kisses her on the cheek, "See you after a while." "Ok Thadeus," replies Ashanti. He walks out the door.

Ashanti goes on with her daily routine of maintaining the plantation. She tries to keep Thadeus off her mind but she can't. The days go by fast because she is busy. The nights seem to drag because she can't sleep and she can't stop thinking about Thadeus. Friday comes and she gets up first thing in the morning. She mounts a horse out the livery stable and takes a quick ride around the interior of the plantation. She notices that everything has been done and there is nothing else left to do. She rides over to the stolen inhabitants living quarters as they are getting up to go to work for the day. Dingo walks up to Ashanti, "Beautiful monin'." Ashanti giggles because as a result of Thadeus constantly correcting her grammar she can now point out bad grammar when others speak. "Yea, it is a nice monin'. There's nothing to do; I guess ya's free day starts today." Dingo reacts and chuckles as if he had just been told that he is finally free. He yells out the news to everyone else and the mood of the workers changes as it becomes obvious that they needed a day to rejoice and party. Dingo comes back to Ashanti happy as a pig in doo doo.

Ashanti takes off heading towards the mansion. Ms. MayBell and Bulla are cleaning the good china and taking inventory of what they have. "Why y'all be doin' this so early?" asks Ashanti, "The ball ain't till free day comin up." "We know," says Bulla, "We just makin' sure everythang be just fine." MayBell looks at Ashanti with a strange look and then says, "We did not see ya's come pass us. How you get in here?"

"I came through the front dowe."

MayBell and Bulla both say at the same time, "Mmmmmm. You'n be havin' some gold down dair." Ashanti throws her head up and walks like a model past MayBell and Bulla. MayBell yells out, "You goan girl!" She tells one of the boys to get the horse which is tied up next to the mansion and bring it to the livery stable. Ashanti goes back to her house where she cleans and rearranges things.

The evening seems to come earlier than usual and Ashanti hears music clearly coming from the stolen people's quarters. MayBell and Bulla knock on Ashanti's door. Ashanti opens the door and MayBell and Bulla say at the same time, "Come on girl, let's goan down an' have us a good one."

"Y'all go on, I'll catch up wit' ya's," replies Ashanti. Ashanti, for some reason stops in front of her mantel that is on the wall and stares at the pouch that she hasn't worn for a while. She picks it up and looks at it hard. *I miss my pouch. I haven't worn it since the first day I came here.* She brings it into the pantry and puts some of the contents that she has in jars on shelves into it. Then she puts it over her head, kissing it before she tucks it under her shirt. Then she starts jogging to catch up with MayBell and Bulla.

"We goan have a good time!" shouts Bulla as her big frame shakes to the music. As they get closer, the music gets louder. When they come around the corner, they see children and grown ups dancing to the music. *Geechee is dancing in front of Dingo, like she owns him. Sam is playing the fiddle, another man is playing a tub with a broom stick coming out of it with strings attached to the stick and the tub. Another man is beating a drum and everyone else is dancing. Another man is playing a small piece of steel that he blows into that is close to his mouth. MayBell and Bulla wave for me to come to the side of one of the cabins and they give me a cup of a liquid solution.* Bulla says, "Now girl, you betta sip dat real slow cuz' it will catch up witcha." *I sip it slow and I quickly start feeling good. This must be their home brew, it be stronger than ours at home. I start reminiscing about the people who are dancing in front of me as they become the villagers in my homeland. I feel a nudge, and it is Tiny dancing in front of me.* Ashanti asks Tiny. "That be the dance you be doin' when the bees be stingin'?" He stops, and looks at Ashanti as if to say, "that's not funny, let's dance." After giving her the look he starts dancing again. Ashanti looks down at the bare feet of Tiny noticing the soil from mother earth covering them the same way mother earth covered the villager's feet in her home land. She hands Tiny the last sip of her home brew. He puts the jar by the porch of the house and begins dancing with her. *The music and dances are a little different from the way we use to do it at home. The rhythm and the feeling of the music is all the same. I danced with Joseph, Tiny and a few other young men in between sips of that home brew.*

What Ashanti is calling home brew is in fact good old Mississippi Moon Shine. *"Poor Dingo is stuck with Geechee who is sitting on his lap almost guarding him from me. He looks at me then looks at her and shrugs his shoulders. She quickly turns around to see what Dingo is doing. As the evening goes on the home brew makes me dance the way I use to in my home land.*

She is filling the party scene with her essence. When this happens the men gather around her mesmerized. Geechee keeps turning around, making sure Dingo isn't watching. Bulla and MayBell and the other available women on the plantation have had enough of Ashanti stealing the spot light. MayBell and Bulla grab Ashanti saying, "We betta get some mo' of dat home brew befo' it be all gone." As they walk away, the men heads all turn Ashanti's way as she passes.

It is getting late as the night is winding down. I am feeling no pain. Bulla and MayBell put me between them and they start walking toward our homes, singing one of the songs that was being played and sung at the party. Geechee and Dingo disappear in the woods. Something I imagine that has happened many times before. Bulla and MayBell continue holding me as we zigzag our way home. They get me to my house and I stumble through the front door and into my bedroom. I feel someone pulling my dress off, and then my panties. I snatch away from whom ever is touching and playing with the parts of me body in which only one man can touch."

"Hold on now Baby Girl, it's me, Thadeus." At this time Ashanti turns in his direction and curls herself in a little ball, so whoever it is, could not take advantage of her. "Now, come on, Baby Girl, come here." Ashanti is not sure at first of who it is until Thadeus strikes a match and lights one of the kerosene lanterns in the room. When she sees it is him, she flops her way into his arms and she hugs him as hard as she can. "Baby Girl, you are tow up from the flow up. I never seen you like this before." Thadeus picks Ashanti up and lays her across her bed and continues taking her clothes off. He takes his clothes off and lays himself down next to her waiting for the first chance he gets to make love to her.

The next morning Ashanti is awaken by the rooster's crowing. She usually hops up and washes herself before going out to make sure the plantation is running correctly. On this morning she cannot quite get up because she has a hangover from the previous night. She hears the front door open and then her bedroom door gets pushed open. It is Thadeus with eggs and pancakes and orange juice. He has bacon on his plate but does not offer her any because he knows from previous experience that Ashanti does not eat pork. She smiles, "Thadeus, I be waitin' for you all night. These days be goin' too slow fo' me, could not wait fo' you to get home." "I could not wait to get home to you." He puts the plates on a small table next to the bed. She hugs him first before she starts eating her food. Ashanti kisses Thadeus while still having jam all over her lips. "Girl, you don't need no jam on yo lips cuz' you got that sweet suga'." Ashanti now understand what Thadeus wants, which is what she wants as well.

They both hurry eating so they can have each other for desert. After the love making is over they both look into each other's eyes slightly sweating from the rising hot Mississippi sun.

"Baby Girl, why it be so cool in here but so hot outside?" It's cooler in here than it is in my home and I have them chaps fan me to sleep every night."

"I do not know, I guess you built me house on the coolest part of our land," "Ashanti, again, not me house, it's my house, say my house."

"Mmy house."

"I don't right know why, but you got the coolest spot around. Now, how did you get so drunk last night?"

"Well, I got up that mornin' and we did er'y thang 'round here and it not be nuttin' else to do, so I tell dem, I mean, them, that they can have some fun." As they are talking Geechee comes in and gets the plates and silverware to be brought inside to get cleaned. She starts to give Ashanti one of her deadly glances, instead she just kind of rolls her eyes and takes the eating utensils back to the house. Before she walks out the door Ashante stops her. "Listen ta what um gonna tell ya miss Geechee; yo wicked thoughts and dirty deeds will come back to ya." Geechee just sucks her teeth and rolls her eyes because her trap is already set. All she needs is Ashanti to fall in it.

"So we played music and we drank and danced till night fall, then I got grunk and MayBell and Bulla walked me home." Thadeus laughed at how Ashanti pronounced drunk. "Baby Girl, it's drunk, not 'grunk," Thadeus, still laughing, "That was a good idea cuz' I was going to allow them to have a little shin dig, cuz' we all been workin' real hard 'round here. That was a good thang you did Ashanti; it keeps up the moral of our peoples." Ashanti rolls her big sexy eyes and gives Thadeus one of her sexy bashful looks that he cannot resist. Ashanti and Thadeus make love and enjoy each other's company for the whole weekend.

That Sunday evening there was something special about their love making. "Baby Girl, I got some company coming in from out of town and I got to stay at my house tonight."

"That's ok. I understand."

"Geechee will have a list of things we have to get so the dance we are having this weekend can be a success. So when you get up in the mornin' come up to the house and see Geechee."

"Ok Thadeus, I will be there."

Ashanti wakes up the next day and thinks to herself. *Dam I got a funny feeling running all through my body. Something is telling me to stay home and go into town another day. I do not want to let Thadeus down so I am going to go any ways. I begin bathing and then I put on my town clothes, which are better than my work clothes, but not as fancy as my God day clothes. I just can't get these bad feelings to leave me.* As she is walking to the livery stable to pick up the wagon and drive it to the back of mansion she thinks. *I will not dare pull it in front of the mansion and allow Geechee, or whoever, to come out of the front door to be picked up. I do that only when I know that no one is coming by to witness me doing so. When I got to the livery stable, Sam is already stirring about. He gets up mighty early for an old man."*

"Where be, I mean, where is the wagon?"

"I got it all ready for you and parked it yonder. I thought it was you dat come got it dis monin." I guess not." They both turn and look up toward the mansion. "There it be, up yonder by the big house," "If it was not you, den who fetched it dis monin?"

When Sam is preaching he speaks perfect english but when he is around whites and the rest of the captives, his english is as bad as the rest of them. Ashanti thinks her english is getting better because Thadeus is always correcting her. She begins walking towards the mansion after she thanks Sam for getting the wagon ready for her. *Something feels funny as I am walking towards the mansion. I turn around and Sam is still watching me walk. He has a weird smile that kinda spooks me. Just as I reach the wagon, Geechee comes out of the back door hurrying me.* "Come on Ashanti, we got a lot to fetch, we be havin' a lot ta do be fo' da big dance!" Ashanti jumps up on the wagon, obeying Geechee's urgency to get into town. "Dat was a good ole time dat we had at our shin dig," says Geechee, "I see you'n like dat moon shine and you be dancin' de night up." Ashanti does not know what to think about Geechee's kindness and her being real chummy with her. She feels something is wrong.

As they pull past the front gates there is an echo of someone yelling. Geechee begins to sing to drown out the sound.

"Did you hear somethin' Geechee?"

"Ah, naw, dat be one of dem hounds. It done ran up on a rabbit, don't mind it."

As they round the corner, Dingo is calling out for them to stop because he is supposed to go with them. Ashanti feels something is wrong and she does not want to go into town. No sooner than they get on down the road Geechee is back to her same non responsive and nasty self. She does not speak to Ashanti until they get into town. Ashanti pulls the wagon in a space in front of the store. Geechee says in an unsure and nervous voice, "Um, Ashanti, Thadeus tell me be fo' he leave, dat dair is two types of feed he need. He tell me you be knowin'what he talkin 'bout. I goan get started wit da stuff we need fo' da house, an' you'n go get da feed."

I pull the wagon down the side of the store and park in front of the feed store. There is a big barn door that is closed, and it would have to open for me to pull in side, in order to pick up the feed. There is a small door that is open for me to walk inside. I walk in yelling. "Hey, is anyone here, hello, hello?" The door immediately slams shut and an ugly familiar face emerges out the shadow behind the closed door. It is Gilbert Poole, who is the owner of this feed store. I sure remember Thadeus talking to Douglas about him. I try to run around him, back out the only entrance I know. He grabs me, slamming me to the ground whispering, 'I gotcha now, you pretty nigra bitch. You come swaying 'round white men like a cat in heat. Um o teach you about eva hittin' a white man and given yo stuff up like niggra hoes suppose' ta.'

I try fighting him, but he is heavy and still has strength in his arms. He tries kissing me, but I turn my head, as he tries to do so over and over again. His breath smells of chewing tobacco and shit. He lifts my dress and rips my panties off and he begins violating me by touching me in places where I only allow Thadeus to touch. It is over as quick as it started. He rolls off me and stands up, pulling his pants up, tucking his shirt into them just as if nothing ever happened. He is out of breath saying, "Now, you bet' not tell Thadeus what happened. If you do, I got some folks 'round here that will string you up in a minute. I done told dem what you did to me and they wanted to go back to Thadeus' place and string you up and him too, if he'n got in the way."

I never felt this bad or hurt in my life. He took something from me that was never his. I don't want anything to happen to Thadeus, so I better not say anything. He did not penetrate me because he arrived before he could stick it in. His fluid on me is as bad as him penetrating me.

Ashanti leaves the torn panties on the floor of the barn. She is not the same person that walked through the door crossing over the thresh hold of one of the worst things that has ever happened to her, other than being enslaved. She jumps in the wagon, slaps the horses with the straps and they take off, rounding the corner, pulling in front of the store where Geechee is waiting. Geechee is standing there, next to a bunch of merchandise that she has bought from the store. She has a devious look on her face as she waits for Ashanti to pull up. Ashanti says nothing to her while two black men help Geechee load the wagon. Ashanti will not say a word to no one, she just pulls off after the wagon gets loaded. Geechee keeps on talking and Ashanti does not answer.

I got the impression of Geechee knowing what happened as soon as she said. "Ol' Mr. Poole, you be havin' to watch out fo' him cuz' one time he take it from me when I not wont to give it to he. He tell me not to talk cuz' he kill me and Thadeus. He thang was as big as," Geechee holds up her pinky. "I be thinking, um, oh, get it good, seein' dat he takin' it but it not be good, so I be mad at him." Ashanti is not sure, but she thinks Geechee has set her up. "I wanted to tell you." "Why didn't you tell me before I went back there?" *That would not have made a difference because I know she wanted it to happen.*" Crossing her arms, Geechee slowly slides back against the back of the seat, like a cobra, reloading before it strikes again.

Chapter X

When they arrive back at the plantation Dingo comes from the side of the mansion waiting for them to pull up. Y'all not hear me callin' y'all?" Ashanti does not speak as Dingo walks next to them as they pull around the corner of the back of the mansion. "I know y'all hear me cuz' Geechee, you turn 'round and see me wavin' y'all to come back." "I ain't see ya." "Yea ya did, and you'n knows I spose to go wit y'all cuz' masta tell us both night befo."

Geechee tries to act surprised but guilt can be seen written all over her face. Then, her look changes from guilt to, "Dam right, I did it." Ashanti knows for a fact that Geechee set her up. The look on Ashanti's face went from being upset to rage. *My monthly will be coming this week. I hope it does because if it does not, that means my baby could be by that dirty bastard. Even though most of him was outside me he could have got some in me."* Ashanti gets off the wagon and quickly runs to her house filled with grief. Not knowing if she is of child and if so, is it the man's she loves or the bastard's she hates?

She stays in her room for the next couple days, not answering the door for any one. Every day that her monthly does not come, she gets more depressed. She finally takes some candles from her shelf and mixes herbs and other material creating a concoction and drinks it. As the candles burn she is on her knees rolling her upper torso around counter clock wise. She yells out 'Zuka Mallie' and goes into a trance and passes out on the floor.

She is awakened by some hard knocks on her door. "Who be knocking at my dowe like that?" "Baby Girl, it's me, Thadeus." Ashanti jumps up and runs to the door, unlocking it as fast as she can. Thadeus walks in and they embrace. "Baby Girl, every one done told me that they ain't seen nor heard from ya." Ashanti forgets what happened to her because of Thadeus's presence, but her expression quickly changes because she is reminded of what happened by the questions Thadeus is asking her. She quickly remembers what she had done the night before so she runs out and looks up into the sky and she sees a rainbow over her house. Thadeus is puzzled over why Ashanti was acting so happy. He went out to see for himself why she is jumping for joy. He looks in the sky and sees the rainbow as well. He begins to scratch his head for two reasons: Ashanti is acting like she has never seen a rainbow before, and it hasn't rained in weeks; he knows that rainbows usually follow a rain storm. *I run back over to Thadeus and hug him as hard as I can. I look into his eyes and say, 'Thadeus, I be, I mean, I am going to have yow baby.' He does not know what to think about the information I just gave him. It takes time before it registers in his brain. Thadeus picks me up and spins me around in the air."*

"Now you know you can't be liftin' and ridin' horses like you do."

"It will be just fine, I will make show things still get done 'round here."

"We got two mo' days before the big ball and we still got a lot of prep work to do. I got to go inta town for some more things. I will be back direca."

Thadeus lets Ashanti go and starts heading back towards the mansion., Ashanti yells out, "Thadeus, who you tell the other day to go into town wit' me."

"I told Geechee and Dingo to go with you. Why?"

"Oh, nothing, I just wonna know."

Now Ashanti knows Geechee set her up. That's all she needed to know. Thadeus remembers what he initially came down to Ashanti's house for. He wanted to know why she stayed in the house for three days, which is not typical of her. She is usually out and about. He turns around and shouts out,

"You sure you ok, Baby Girl? You got something I need to know?"

"No, no, Thadeus, I am just fine, I got a lot of work to do. I will see you later."

After seeing Thadeus come from the house, Bula and MayBell walk towards Ashanti's house. When they arrive Bulla knocks on the door and Ashanti opens it.

"Come on in MayBell, Bulla."

The two women step in to ask Ashanti, "Are you'n all right? cuz' we see Geechee mighty happy 'round the house, and you not be comin' out."

Bulla steps to Ashanti looking into her eyes and says, "Shanti, now, what dat girl done to you?"

Ashanti starts to tear up and Bulla puts her arms around her hugging and consoling her. "She send me back behind the stowe to the feed barn to fetch some special grain Thadeus told her for me to pick up."

"And?"

"He take it from me."

"She be dirty as a rattle snake."

"I thought she was y'alls friend girl, cuz' y'all be together 'ginst me."

"She kinda had us 'ginst you, but dat not last dat long cuz' we remember the dirt she do to us. We be here befo' Geechee and when she come here from Na Orlens she keep up a lot of mess. Having me and MayBell fighten' and arguing wit 'each udda. Thadeus ain't pay us much 'tention since she be here. We be glad you come here so she get what we got." They both hug Ashanti and become a mass of women and humility.

For the next couple of days everyone is cleaning up and prepping the plantation for the grand ball that is to take place the coming Saturday. *I have not seen Geechee around. It seems as though she is avoiding me, guilty of what she has done to me. When I finally catch up to her, she does not give me her usual nasty look. She puts her head down and scurries past me like a scolded dog that just got hollered at by its master; further revealing her guilt for what happened to me.*

It's the big day and everything is in its place. Joseph and Tiny have suit jackets on, knickers with shiny black shoes and white stocking up to their knees. I and the rest of the women in the house have black dresses with white aprons and white stockings with black shoes. Dingo and two other men all have suits on just like Joseph and Tiny. Dingo and the two other men park the buggies or direct the drivers where to park. The big ball room has been cleaned and polished and it sparkles. Everyone who arrives is announced by their Griot to make a grand entrance. I imagine myself and Thadeus being announced by the same Griot as we make our grand entrance. My dream gets interrupted by a nudge from Bulla. "Girl, you got to walk 'round here handin Champaign to folks." *The band plays and the people begin to dance and enjoy themselves. The music is not like the music that was played at the shin dig we had here or in my home land and they do not dance the way we do either. The rhythm is missing from the music and from their bodies."*

The griot announces the next couple. "Mr. and Mrs. Poole." *He walks in with his fat wife and his stinking shit breath. He sees me out of the corner of his eye and I can tell by the look on his face that I make him uncomfortable. The dance goes on and the people eat and drink the night away. After I make my rounds with the glasses of champaign, I wait at the entrance of the ball room where I keep the tray of drinks. Gilbert makes his way around to where I am at and stands next to me. He talks out the side of his mouth.* "You aint tell nobody cuz' you know what I'll do to ya."

Now, I ain't said nothin to nobody, I just be wonderin, when will I get some again? Cuz' you made me feel so good down there."

He grins at what Ashanti just said. The fear of Thadeus knowing what happened quickly wipes the grin away.

"Well, you know, we can't get caught talkin' cuz' people might be looking at us now."

"I got an idea so they not know, stay here."

Ashanti goes in the kitchen and pulls out her pouch and mixes some ingredients in a bowl and pours them into a glass of punch. She says her favorite incantation, ending with "Zuka Mallie". She immediately walks back to where Mr. Poole is standing, hoping that he is still there. He is there, just like a male dog in heat waiting to get some. "I hand him the drink and tell him, See, ain't nobody goan think anything; they just see me bring you something special to drink. I be comin' inta town in a few days. I cane't wait, I got juices flowing down my leg like the same way you got that drink flowing down yo throat."

Mr. Poole chokes a little at the thought of what Ashanti just said as he walks over toward Thadeus to talk. Ashanti looks on hoping that he finishes his drink, which he does. Nate walks up to Thadeus and says, Thadeus everyone that is someone is here: Eddingtons, Richardsons, Godbolts, Braceys, Hueys, Braxtons, Hodges, Bradfords, Bonds, Cottons, Jacksons and a whole heap more." Dang Ol Nate ya dam near named everyone." Thadeus pats Nate on the back as they both laugh as Thadeus walks away to host his grand ball.

The dance is winding down and the last of the guests are gone. Geechee, Bulla, MayBell and Ashanti begin cleaning up. Thadeus yells out, "Leave that be until the morning! Y'all did enough work for the day." They all begin to walk back to their sleeping quarters when Thadeus grabs Ashanti's hand and asks her, "My dear, may I have this dance?" as he bows while asking. "I courtesies

to him the same way I saw the women at the ball earlier do. Yes, you may."
He puts one arm around my waist and the other arm in the air as he spins me
around the room to the beat of imaginary music in the air." *We do not have to go
into town for a while. I just said that to Mr. Poole so I could get him to drink.*

The doctor came by a few weeks after the ball and Ashanti overhears him
and Thadeus talking. "Thadeus, I come by here to get that remedy that puts old
animals to sleep, that your girl has."

"Oh yea, not a problem doc, she will be back here in a few."

"That was some good time we had at y'alls ball. It was as good as when
yo daddy use ta have them when you were knee high to a grass hopper." "Oh
yea, you know that Gillbert Poole died yesterday?"

"No, I didn't know that."

"Yea, he was walking around in a zombie like state for days. People say
his wife did something to him, cuz' she knows he goes around trying to sow
his oats like a bitch dog in heat. I went to check on him a few times but I did
not know what to make of it. His wife says that he started eating everything in
sight like he never ate before. She found him the next day dead."

"What, he ate himself to death?"

"No, He defecated all over the back room. He slept there because his
wife would not sleep with him anymore. Apparently he began eating his own
shit and he choked on it."

"Dam, what a way ta go doc!"

"Yea Thadeus, it's a turrible thang."

Ashanti listens to the conversation grinning as the doctor ends the
story. She skips in the room like a child that is on her way to buy some candy.
Ashanti gives the doctor a small pouch and says, "Mix two teaspoons of this in
water and the animal will die with no pain or suffering." "Thank ya Baby Girl.
You sure you don't want to give me yo recipe for this potion?" Thadeus inter-
venes, "Now doc, you know we cane't give you our recipe. It's a Wellington's
secret." The doctor climbs back up on his buggy and his black servant snaps
the reigns and they take off.

Sam continues to hear the children mention the names of the Gods
Ashanti has told them about, especially Guanab, which the children call
'gwanna,' using that name as a threat to someone being, or doing bad deeds.
Ashanti continues to do the work around the plantation as her child swells her

belly. Sam is ready to get rid of her because as he says, "Ashanti is turning my people inta heathens."

Ashanti is walking past the livery stable. Sam quietly gets her attention by waving his arms and saying, "Pssssst." Ashanti sees and hears Sam and starts walking his way. He looks around to make sure no one is around to hear them.

"Ashanti, you are starting to show," as he touches her stomach.

"Yea, I can't wait till he comes out. He is actin' like he be ready now."

Sam looks around again to make sure no one hears them. "Ashanti, I know you don't want that chap to be born a slave." Ashanti has a shocked look on her face. It never dawned on her that her child would be born into bondage.

"No Sam, I not want that."

"Well, I know how you can get away and yo child not be born a slave."

"How can I get away from 'round here?"

"Well, it be time real soon that we have to pick and bale the cotton. It got to be loaded on trains to go up north. I got some peepas that work on the train and they will make a space for ya."

Ashanti allows the words that come from Sam's mouth to resonate through her mind. She loves Thadeus and at the same time she does not want her child to be born a slave.

"Well, you'n think about what I said, and if you want ta go, I will tell me peepas to set you a spot on one of the cars."

Ashanti nods and continues to walk back toward her house. What Sam has said continues to run through her mind. She does not want her child born into bondage and at the same time she really loves Thadeus. She looks towards the slave quarter and watches as Thadeus orders two young children to take some tools he just bought to the workers in the field. That instantly made her not want her child born into slavery. She starts walking back toward the livery stable. She is almost there when Sam walks out. She looks at Sam and nods 'ok'. Sam instantly knows what she wants to do. He nods back 'yes,' signifying that he understands that she wants to stow away. Ashanti turns around and heads back toward her house. Thadeus is walking towards her and she just gives him a half smile and walks into her house. He continues past her house and stops to talk to Sam.

"Sam, what done got into Baby Girl? She just looked at me like I getting her pregnant ruined her life."

"Naw masta I think it mean mo den dat."

"What you mean Sam?"

"I overheard some of the field hands and her talkin."

"About what? Spit it out."

"I heard Dingo and Ashanti, and some of the udens say they goan stow away up north on the train when they load it with cotton."

"I don't believe that."

"You know that Dingo got a thang for Ashanti. I mean, Baby Girl, and she don't want her chap born a slave."

"I still don't believe that."

"Well, you see the way she just acted wit' ya."

"I still can't believe it."

"Just keep yo eyes and ears open."

"I will do just that." Replies Thadeus

"Sam you be one of the oldest we have 'round here."

"I trust what you are saying but I hope that you are wrong."

Thadeus's plantation is just about three weeks away from loading the box cars on the train with cotton. Ashanti does not spend a lot of time in or around Thadeus. It is not because she does not like him; it is because she has not been in the mood since she became impregnated. Thadeus is starting to believe Sam, even though he does not want to. The free workers of Thadeus's plantation have picked the cotton and brought it to another barn where it is made into bails. Thadeus has to get some of his brother's wagons to get all his cotton onto the box cars in town. He looks at Ashanti and says, "Girl, I got to go. I'm going to count on you to get this cotton in ta town." She hugs him and he kinda pushes her off.

I don't know why he's acting like this toward me. I aint did him no kinda way. Well, I got work ta do. I ain't studying him. We bailed up the cotton then we loaded them on the wagons. Sam yells, "Hold up, y'all I goin' wit' y'all!" *Sam never leaves the plantation, something just ain't right. We get into town and start loading the bails onto the box cars. Sam motions with his head to one of the box cars where I would stow away. Dingo and a few others ask me if they could come with me. I know something is wrong. I look for Sam and he is nowhere to be found. I definetly know now that something is wrong. I told Dingo to tell the others that something ain't right. Let's just get back into the wagons and go back to the plantation."*

As the train is pulling off, they are getting back into the wagon to head back home. Ashanti looks under the box cars and see a bunch of horse legs as they pass.

"Hold up everybody, look yonder under da train!"

As the last car passes there are men sitting on horseback waiting, and one of them is Thadeus. I wave at him and he half waves back to me with a big smile on his face. I wave my hand again as a signal to move out. We have our own wagon train heading back towards the Plantation. I know that Sam set me up, but I'm going to act like nothing happened. Sam and I got business to take care of, in due time, IN DUE TIME! Thadeus is over joyed to know that his baby is not going to try to leave him.

Chapter XI

Days go by and those days turned into months. The work of the summer has come to an end. During these times the captured laborers have to provide for themselves by hunting and fishing while the women can the vegetables they grew in the garden to make it through the winter. Douglas, Thadeus's brother, would often use them on his small plantation that he owns not too far from the Wellington's estate. Ashanti's stomach also reflects the passage of time. Thadeus spends many nights lying with Ashanti rubbing her stomach as they comfort each other with their presence on these cool Mississippi nights.

One morning, a conversation with MayBell and Bula gets interrupted as Geechee comes around the corner, holding her stomach. "Bulla, these cramps be killin' me. I cane't take dem no mo." "Well Geechee, you betta go ask Shanti to fix you up somethin'." Geechee looks up at Bulla with discomfort reflected on her face.

"Bulla, you know dat gal not like me much. Tell she it be fo' you."

"Ok Geechee, it be fo' me. Come see me lata and I give it to ya's."

Not too long after their conversation, Ashanti comes waddling in the back door of the plantation. Ashanti is met by Bulla while she is coming through the back door of the mansion. "Ashanti, I be needin' somthin' fo' my cramps. Ya know, it be dat time of the month fo' me."

As Bulla is speaking, she is winking her eye at Ashanti. Ashanti instantly knows who the potion is for. "Ok Bula. I fix it right up for ya's, I'll be back direca." As Ashanti is speaking to Bulla she winks her eye back at her, turns around and waddles back out the door heading back towards her home to fix Geechee something for her cramps, which makes Ashanti smile from ear to ear.

Ashanti walks into her house heading straight for her shelves which are full of jars filled with herbs and other things she has gathered from the woods and purchased from the store. She pours some of the herbs she has stored into a bowl, then pours some more ingredients into the bowl she got from her pouch. She begins mixing the ingredients in the wooden bowl, chanting as she mixes them. She shouts out, "Zooka Mallie!" and the mixing stops. She pours the content of the bowl into a cup and starts waddling back towards the door while humming "wade in the water, wade in the water, children." When Ashanti reaches the back door of the mansion, Bulla opens the door. Ashanti hands Bulla the cup and they both thank each other, winking at each other at the same time. Ashanti quickly turns around and says, "Bulla, you must drink it down immediately for it to work."

"Ok Shanti, I will do just dat."

Geechee hears everything and walks toward Bulla and snatches the drink from her hand. "You ain't have to take it like dat."

"Ah, go pluck some chickens!"

Geechee says that while switching her curvy body and drinking the concoction down and frowning up from the taste of it. Bulla face changes from a frown for the way Geechee snatched the cup to a menacing smile, knowing that she just drank the concoction of Ashanti's revenge. In minuets Geechee cramps go away.

Geechee went to bed early and she got up early the next day. She rose up into a sitting position, allowing the cover to drop down from her chest to her waist. There is an odor of death coming from between Geechee's legs. It is so foul that Geechee cannot take the smell herself. Her face frowns from the smell. MayBell opens Geechee's door to tell her something and her face frowns from the smell as well. MayBell backs out of the room with a terrible expression on her face. Thadeus happens to be walking by and sees the look on MayBell's face. He opens the door and sticks his head in. When the scent hits him he yells out, "Dam Geechee, what up in the hell got up in you?" Geechee slips back down in her bed with her foul smell. The foul smell coming from Geechee is a combination of rotton eggs and sulfur from a freshly lit match.

Ashanti stays in her home rubbing her belly waiting for a sign that her potion has worked. She stands at her window, looking towards the mansion. One of the young boys comes into Ashanti's home and puts more wood on the fire to keep Ashanti warm and cozy. She continues rubbing her belly and looking out her window towards the mansion on this chilly Mississippi morning. Ashanti sees Bulla running out the door waving one of her arms frantically while the other holds a shawl around her neck. Just before she knocks on the door, Ashanti opens the door, welcoming Bulla into her home.

"Shanti, you may hafta make Geechee somethin for that bad smell coming from she thang, cuz' it smell somethin' awful."

"She ain't getting' nawn nothin' from me."

Bulla begins to laugh at what Ashanti just said.

"I had to come here and tell you what happen. I must be gettin' own back to fix Thadeus' breakfast. Ashanti grabs Bulla arm and tells her. "Don't say me be getting back, say I must be getting back"

Bulla smiles at Ashanti and says, "I must be gettin' back."

"Also Bulla Geechee ain't done wit' me workin' my pain on her."

Bulla shakes her head, grips the shawl around her neck to reintroduce herself to the chill of the morning. Geechee is sitting up on her bed, still wondering how she got the foul odor between her legs.

"I ain't did nothing no different from what I usually do ery day." Geechee tells herself, "I did not itch or have any foul smell coming from there. My monthly is over and I have a little smell before I take a cleanin down there but not this bad." Her expression changes as if a light has just turned on inside her head. "I had that stuff I drank from Baby Girl. That be the only thang I did different. How did Ashanti know it was for me, I know Bulla did not tell Ashanti it was for me. I think that girl done hoodooed me! I got the right mind to cut she throat!" Little does Geechee know that the smell will be the least of her worries.

Ashanti waddles up to the mansion to see or, should we say, smell for herself the damage her potion has caused. Ashanti gets inside the mansion and knocks on Geechee's door.

"Come in."

Ashanti sticks her head in the door and scowls at the stench. "How you doin' Geechee?"

"Don't you how you doin' me bitch. I aint done nuttin I ain't usually do, but drink dat stuff you made."

"What stuff? I ain't made nothing for you. I made Bulla somethin' for her cramps. I don't know what you be talkin bout."

"I knows ya put something own me; I just knows it."

"I can make sometin' to fix it, if ya want me to."

"Hell naw, get the hell way from me, ya hoodoo bitch!"

"I don't know what you talkin 'bout." says Ashanti as she closes the door with a smile on her face. *She ain't felt nothing yet, till her monthly be over with. She helped take something from me that was not hers to give, so I'm going to scar her for life.*

Geechee's monthly is over and she sneaks out to the big oak tree to meet Dingo for one of their rendezvous. It is chilly outside, so they head for the barn that has the warmth of hay. They kiss and he lays Geechee on the hay and slowly starts pulling her panties down. The lower he pulls them down the more the smell starts to ease out of her panties until the smell becomes unbearable for Dingo to take. "Dam Geechee, what up in da hell got inta you?" His large member shrinks from the smell, like a seedling wilts from being in the mid-day sun. Dingo rises to his feet, backing away from Geechee. As he is backing up he begins to say, "Geechee, you'n have the smell of death down dair, you ain't passin' dat to me." As he backs away from Geechee his pace quickens to get away from her stench. She yells out, "No baby, you be de only joyment' I be havin' 'round here. No baby, not you!" Geechee slowly gets up from being dissed by Dingo. As she walks by Ashanti's home she wants to throw a rock through her window. She goes to bed with revenge on her mind.

Next day she wakes up and heads toward the kitchen to the outhouse to relieve herself. As she walks down the hall she sees Bulla and MayBell gossiping like they do most mornings when she gets up. The expression on their faces changes as they look at Geechee.

"What's wrong? Why y'all be lookin at me like dat?" demands Geechee in a rude tone.

Bulla points at Geechee's mouth, "What be dat 'round yo mouth?"

Geechee feels around her mouth and feels bumps with fluid oozing out of them. She runs down the hall and looks in one of the full sized mirrors on the wall and she starts screaming. She feels down around her private area and feels the same fluid oozing bumps, which make her scream even louder. Meanwhile, Ashanti is in her house rubbing her stomach, looking out her window, she listens to the screams, a product of her revenge, which makes her smile. She hears a knock on the door. It is a woman with a child that is screaming from being sick. She brought the child for Ashanti to doctor on. Ashanti rubs something on the child's chest and something in its nostrils. The child sneezes and instantly starts smiling which brings a different type of smile upon Ashanti's face.

The second trauma that happened to Geechee comes a few days before her monthly and lasts for a few days after it ends. She wears a hat that has a veil with holes for her eyes cut out covering her face to hide her bumps. MayBell and Bulla beg Ashanti to give her something to stop the smell because it is unbearable and they can't take it anymore. Thadeus is going to put her in the field but Bulla and MayBell beg him not to because they do not want to share her duties around the mansion. Finally Ashanti gives her something that lessens the smell and makes the bumps heal faster.

Days continue to get colder which Ashanti does not like at all. She comes into the house and she notices Bulla and MayBell pulling silver and gold material out of a closet. "What are y'all doing and what is all this," as she touches a piece of the silver material. Well Thadeus likes us to put up our Christmas tree a month earlier to get the Christmas spirit," Replies Bulla. What is Christmas?" Asks Ashanti with a confused look on her face. It is the day Jesus Christ was born and on that day we give each other gifts. You know Christ the man Sam be talkin' 'bout on God day. Yes I know Jesus, he be the man who the white people say they love and want to live like and they treat us like cattle. I just don't get it, Christmas, Thanksgiving and we still living in hell." Ashanti leaves the mansion shaking her head in disbelief. Days go by and Thadeus is doing a lot of sneaking around. Ashanti stops him and asks. "Thadeus what done got into you? You come over and stay the night and all but you gone a lot during the day; aint no real work to do 'round here, where you be?" "Well girl I just got things ta do." Thadeus turns away and scurries on about his business. He turns back around and yells out. "Did you see the tree, mighty fine isn't it?" Ashanti shakes her head and goes back into her house.

Thadeus is not like most slave masters. He gives all his slaves something for Christmas. Every Christmas Eve he gathers everyone around the same big oak tree they go to on God day to exchange gifts. The lower branches of the tree are decorated with silver and gold just like the one in the mansion. The only difference is that this tree is alive and being used all year round. This year Ashanti will take part in the celebration. It is Christmas eve and they all gather around the big Oak tree singing come all ye faithful passing gifts to each other and drinking eggnog. Bulla, MayBell and Geechee leave before the festivities are over.

Thadeus walks behind Ashanti and puts his arms around her softly grasping her belly, saying, "Baby Girl this be my favorite day of the year, I am so glad I am spending it with you." Ashanti is thinking about all the celebrations being held and her people are still slaves. "I see you handin out gifts, where is mines?" Thadeus pats Ashanti on her stomach and says. "Here's your gift from me." Ashanti sarcastically laughs, "Hahaha." Thadeus turns her around to ask her. "What do you want?" Ashanti looks up in the star lit sky and thinks, "My freedom."

They turn and slowly walk back towards Ashanti's home. As they get closer she notices more lights than usual in her house. When they get to her house she wobbles quickly up the steps into her home and sees a big well lit Christmas tree with gifts all around it. She turns and faces Thadeus. Thank you, but I don't have anything for you." Thadeus smiles and says, "Yes Baby Girl you did give me something." "What?" "You." They hug each other and Ashanti begins tearing the gift wrap off her presents like a child experiencing their first Christmas.

At the end of February, Ashanti gives birth to her first child which is a baby boy. *He has the same twinkle in his eye that Thadeus had when I first met him. So I named him Thad. He is very curious and seems to understand me when I talk to him. Shortly after having my son I got pregnant again. This time I had a girl. I named her Bernita, she reminds me of myself. She has big round eyes and dimples. Shortly after having her, Thadeus got me pregnant again. He takes time with his children, somewhat as a father should, but looks at them very strangely. Almost as if he is looking at them like they would one day make him a lot of money.*

One day Ashanti tells Thadeus, "Thadeus, you ain't gonna be treatin' my children like you do the rest of these chaps 'round here."

"I know." he replies, "These be my chaps and I know how I'm going to treat them."

"How?"

"Just like the rest of my chaps. They gonna have special work and know the value of hard work."

Ashanti looks at him as if to say, "I hear you, but you ain't gonna be slaving my children like you do your other children."

Ashanti gave birth every year for the next eight years. She had Wilburt, Benjamin, Jerry, Oliver, Jacquline, Charlene, Janice, Donna and Joseph. Ashanti teaches them everything Mojo taught her. They are all natural leaders in their own right. Young Thadeus spends a lot of time with Sam, learning everything he can from him. He began to hang around the livery stable just after he learned how to walk.

Chapter XII

The years continue to pass and the children are growing and learning. Ashante thinks to herself. *Thadeus has been acting funny as if he is hiding something. He has not been coming to my house as often as he used to and when he does, it's not to make love to me. He avoids eye contact with me and every time I try looking into his eyes, he just looks away. If there is one that Thadeus has taken up with, I know it's me who he really loves.*

Ashanti goes to the mansion and notices that Bulla and MayBell are trying to avoid her and cannot look her in the eye. Geechee walks past Ashanti with a shit eating grin. Ashanti knows something is wrong; she just can't put her finger on it. *One day I saw a young white woman looking out the back door of the mansion. Then, she stepped out, looking all around as if she was surveying her land. She turned around and went back into the house. I hollered down to the livery stable for Thad to come home. When he got here I told him to watch his sisters and brothers until I get back. I started walking toward the mansion to see for myself what was going on. As I walk through the back door, Bulla turns around quickly and acts like she was too busy to speak to me. I did not say anything to her because I am not going to force no one to do something if they don't want to. As I walk out of the kitchen, Geechee starts laughing at the sight of me.*

"What's ticklin' you so?"

"Now you goan be knowin' how I felt when you came along. Masta stop takin' up wit' me when you came along. Masta got hitched to a white woman. She be promised to him when he was a lidda chap. I know you know how to work a Mojo," Geechee laughs as she is talking, "Well, you best work a mojo on yo' own stuff, to get him back."

Ashanti also starts laughing as she speaks, "I don't need to work no mojo on my stuff, all he need to do is get some and he will do to her what he did to you. When he gets some of this again, it will make him forget all about hers. I ain't worried cuz' I made him be what he is today. Too bad I can't say the same about you cuz' yo stuff stanks and its bumpy and pussie." Ashante is now in her late thirties and still has a raw and sexy body even though she has had a lot of children.

Ashanti turns around and starts walking towards the kitchen leaving out the back door. Her words have smacked Geechee's smile right off her face. She is enraged by what Ashanti just said and Ashante begins to think about what Geechee just told her.

I don't care that Thadeus is married, that marriage was arranged when I was in my home land. Those arranged marriages happen in my home land as well. Thadeus should know not to avoid me cuz' I understand everything he brings to me. As long as he does not disrespect me cuz' of her, everything will be just fine. Every morning Thadeus goes to the north pasture to make sure his workers are working. I usually stop by to do the same thing before going back to see after my children. He goes back up to the mansion to have breakfast. I will be waiting for him at the back door.

Early the next morning Ashanti heads toward the mansion to meet Thadeus when he arrives. "Bulla has the kitchen smelling great. She looks me in the eye because she knows what I am about to do." Thadeus walks in the back door where Ashanti is waiting. Ashanti pushes him back out the back door and hems him against the back wall of the mansion.

"Why you been avoiding me Thadeus?"

"Uh uh um um."

"I don't care if you have a wife, just don't dis me fo she."

"I wanted to tell you Baby Girl, but I just didn't know how."

"They had those types of marriages in my home land, I understand. Don't you ever ignore me like that again! You hear me Thadeus?"

"Yes Baby Girl"

Ashanti lets Thadeus go and starts proceeding toward her home. She turns around and shouts, "Don't be negletin this stuff too long, it might get cob webs down there!"

Thadeus smiles as he turns around and walks back into the mansion. Thadeus starts coming to see Ashanti again, making love to her a couple times a week, some weeks even more.

Ashanti finds out that Thadeus' wife is named Margaret but everyone calls her Missy. She is twenty five, seven years older than Ashanti when she first came to the plantation. She is short with blond hair and beautiful blue eyes. She is kinda cute but she is skinny as a string bean, with no meat on her bones. *Ashanti says to herself. Thadeus must really like her for her looks, cuz' she ain't got no body.*

Missy has noticed that Thadeus has not been making love to her lately the way he used to. She knows that Thadeus has a lot of children by Ashanti. She found this out thanks to Geechee, who loves to gossip. Missy stops Geechee at the bottom of the left side of the double staircase to hear the gossip of the day.

"How ya doing Geechee, what's good?"

"Not much Missy, just doin' a day's work."

"Thadeus don't be lovin' me much lately."

"Not tell Thadeus I told you dis, but Thadeus be goin' back and gettin' Baby Girl stuff. She tell me dat if he get she stuff one mo' ginn, then he forget yo'ns. Don't say I told ya, k?"

"Don't worry about it, I won't tell him nothin."

Missy walks back upstairs thinking, "I know Thadeus ain't taking no black nigga slave girl over me, I just know better than that." To reassure herself she sends Geechee to go get Ashanti for her. "Tell that Baby Girl bitch to carry her ass here."

These words make Geechee smile as she is on her way to get Ashanti.

"Yes mam, I be on my way atta her."

Geechee goes to Ashanti's home first, where she runs into one of the older female workers on the planation who is watching Baby Girls' chaps. She tells Geechee to go to the barn where Ashanti went to deliver a calf. Geechee walks into the barn and taps Ashanti on the shoulder and says, "Missy be wantin' ta see ya." Ashanti replies, "Ok, I will go up there after I deliver this calf." Geechee taps her on the shoulder again. "Missy wants you right now."

"Geechee, you bet' not touch me again. Now, I done told you I will be up there after I finish delivering this calf."

Geechee sucks her teeth as if to say, "Who the hell are you, not listenin ta masta's wife," as she heads back to the mansion. Geechee tells Missy, "Mam I done told she two times dat you be wanna ta see she."

"Not see she, it's see her."

"Dat you wanna see her."

"You tell that nigga bitch to get up here right now cuz' she don't want me to come down there and get her because she will get the worst whipping of her life!"

Geechee goes back to the barn and tells Ashanti just what Missy said. Ashanti laughs, *She ain't going to put a hand on me. If Thadeus finds out that she got in the way of making him money, he will be very mad at her. Thadeus ain't never put his hands on me and would not allow no one else to either.*

Ashanti is too valuable to the Plantation, and Thadeus loves her to death. Ashanti gets finished delivering the calf, so she washes up and heads toward the mansion. Ashanti walks into the kitchen down the hall and meets Missy standing in front of the double stair case. Missy steps towards Ashanti,

"Don't you eva, eva not come to me right away when I send for you! You hear me?"

Ashanti would not answer her, she just stands there with her arms crossed rolling her eyes and sucking her teeth sighing as if to indicate that she is bored. Missy begins walking around Ashanti, like she was an officer giving one of her soldiers an inspection.

"Oh, I see, you one of those uppity niggras. Thadeus done knocked you up a bunch of times and he done ruined you. Yo old black pussy ain't got nothing on mines."

Ashanti sighs, "Are you finished with me yet miss missy, cuz' I have another calf to deliver. Thadeus ain't going to be happy when he finds out you messin' with his animals, which is his money."

"Yea, you can go back to your kind. That cow is an animal just like you. And my stuff is better than yours!" Ashanti turns around and says, "If it ain't good, it get old fast, and when it's good, it stay young. You will know, when he night after night drop down next to you and say he too tired to get it up."

Ashanti smirks as she heads back down the long hall leading to the back door towards the barn. Thadeus does not make love to Missy like he used to. He came into the bed room one night, washed up and quietly slid in the bed not to wake Missy. Missy had been waiting for him, so she turns around and puts her hands into his underwear to get him aroused. He gently pulls her hand off his private part and kisses her on the head and says, "Missy, baby, I'm too tired tonight and I have to get up early in the morning." He kisses her on the forehead again before turning the opposite way, laying on his side and goes to sleep. Missy began thinking, "I know he ain't chose no darkey over me, I just know it. I will see what he does for the next few nights."

Missy starts wearing sexy night gowns and provocative perfume. Still, he does not make advances on her. She wonders why he is paying her no mind. "I always bathe, smell good and dress really nice. Why won't he make love to me?" Missy is saying this while looking at herself in the mirror brushing her hair. "I just know he ain't taking that darkey over me. That thought is out of the question, I don't know why it comes into my mind. I am going to check and see for myself."

Missy hears Thadeus approaching on his horse. She looks out the window and watches as Thadeus hands his horse to one of his boys to be brought back to the barn. He looks around to see if anybody is watching. He quickly looks up towards his bedroom to make sure Missy does not see him. She is peeking out the window and ducks down so he cannot see her. She slowly comes back to the window as he starts walking towards the back of the mansion. Missy runs down the stairs and then peeks out the back door, where she sees him going towards his Baby Girl's house. Ashanti's house is the first house before you pass the barns and livery stable where they shoe the horses.

The sun is setting and there is just enough sun light to see. Missy creeps behind Thadeus as he walks towards Ashanti's house. To Missy's horror, Thadeus is met by Ashanti at her door. She kisses Thadeus and rolls her eyes at Missy as she pulls him in making him disappear behind her front door. Missy is furious at what she has just seen and starts walking toward Ashanti's front door. She suddenly stops as she thinks about how important Ashanti really is to the plantation. "Thadeus may be seeing Ashanti to discuss plantation business. I better get back to the house so I can get ready for him," Missy thinks.

She hurries back to the house. When she arrives she calls Geechee,

"Geechee, Geechee, fix me some bath water and put some of those beads in it!"

Missy climbs into the water and begins bathing herself. When she gets out she is dried off by Geechee. After she is dried off she sits down in front of the mirror as Geechee brushes her hair. When her hair is done being brushed, Geechee sprays sweet smelling perfume all over her body. She then climbs in the bed and waits for Thadeus to come. Thadeus comes in the house a few minuets later and asks Geechee to pour hot water in a face bowl. He undresses and starts washing up.

He climbs into bed and Missy jumps on him, kissing and rubbing all over him. "I want you so bad baby, make love to me please," says Missy in a lustful tone of voice. Thadeus pushes Missy off him saying, "Now, I done told you girl, Um tired, leave me be!" Missy backs off Thadeus with pain in her heart, still feeling very horny. She waits until Thadeus is a sleep and slides down to smell his private. She gets very disappointed from finding out that Thadeus's private part smells of a woman. She immediately sees in her mind Ashanti's face rolling her eyes, with a bold and dominate expression on her face; Missy puts her face in her pillow and begins to cry.

Chapter XIII

The next morning Missy arrives at the breakfast table. She is waiting to get enough nerve to speak what is on her mind. She looks at Thadeus and says, "Why is that bitches house so close to ours? Why she ain't with the rest of your nigga slaves?" "What the hell you talkin' 'bout girl? She is in the middle of everything so she can take care of everything. If, and when you can do that, I will put her back by the others. Until then, don't worry about where she is. You need only to worry about where you are. Na hush yow mouth."

Missy jumps up with tears in her eyes and runs upstairs. Thadeus wipes his mouth and walks out the back door on his way to Ashanti's house. He walks in the front door where Ashanti is sitting in her rocking chair with one of their children, rocking him to sleep. He grabs his child and lays him in one of the bed rooms. He comes back in front of Ashanti and picks her up out of her rocking chair guiding her towards her bedroom. She stops him and says, "Now Thadeus, you been coming over here day in and day out. You ain't spent much time with your wife. You been coming here, yay, 'bout every day. You won't be doing me no kinda way by giving yo wife some ding ding."

"But Ashanti, ain't much to her and it don't feel as good as yours,"

"Well, think about me when you go up in her," Ashanti smiles as she is saying this.

"Baby Girl, you one in a million, ain't nobody like you," he says this as he hugs Ashanti and kisses her on the forehead before leaving.

He comes back in his house and goes upstairs, taking his clothes off, and climbs in the bed to make love to Missy. When he puts his arm around her she pushes him off screaming hysterically with tears coming out her eyes. "You better go back there and fuck yo nigga slave bitch! You ain't gettin' none of this good white stuff no mo. I Know you been fucking her cuz' I followed you one evening to her house; then you came back in the bed with me and I smelled you when you fell asleep and you smelled of her. Don't you ever put your hands on me again, you go back there and fuck yo bitch." Thadeus gets up, gets dressed, and does just that. This time he stays all night and throughout the day with Ashanti.

Thadeus stops having sex with Missy all together. One morning Missy gets up and takes a walk around the plantation. She frowns up as she passes Ashanti's house. Shortly after passing Ashanti's house she sees a path in the woods. She turns into the woods and starts walking down the path. Something stops her in her tracks. It is Dingo taking a piss. Missy is in shock because his member reaches almost to his knees. After seeing Dingo's manhood, Missy walks up to him. He flicks the excess piss off and put his rifle back in his pants.

Missy says, "Get over here boy. No, no, no; don't put it back, I want to see it."

He walks toward her, full of fear in his heart and in his mind.

"What's your name boy?" as she looks into his eyes, then down toward his crotch.

"My name be Dingo."

"Well Dingo I want to see what you got down there. Now, pull it back out."

"No, no, no, Missy, masta will kill me."

"Well, if you don't, I'm going to tell him you raped me, so you choose."

Dingo's head droops down as she leads him farther in the woods to have sex. Every time Thadeus leaves, Missy goes and gets Dingoed.

Geechee finds out and hopes Thadeus catches wind of it. Since Geechee herself cannot have any, she doesn't want anybody else to have any of her Dingo. Missy, on the other hand, prefers to do it in the barn, so every time, before they go in the barn, she tells old Sam and Ashanti's oldest son, who is Sam's apprentice, not to come in the barn because she is taking care of business. Dingo always come around the side of the barn and climbs through the window. At the end of the month Missy missed something that always comes, that did not come this time. Thadeus will kill both of them if he finds out that she has been impregnated by Dingo. One morning Geechee comes to Missy's bedroom where she lays sulking and sad.

"Well Missy, I'z know you in some trubba and I'z comes to help ya. I know you ain't had yo monthly and you'n in trubba. I knows someone who can help ya."

Missy jumps out of her bed grabbing Geechee and saying, "Who, who can help me? You better not tell Thadeus about none of this."

"I ain't and nobody else is."

"What you mean nobody else is?."

"Erey one be knowin' 'bout you and Dingo. You not hide it good fo' no one not to know. Masta would kill anyone who tell him, so no one not say nothin' bout it."

"Well, who can help me?"

"Baby Girl can mix you up something to fix it. Ya see, she be da daughter of an medicine man back where she come from."

"I don't believe in that voodoo stuff, and besides, Baby Girl would not help me, she hates me."

"Dat not be da truth, cuz' I hear she when she tell Bulla and MayBell, dat she tell Thadeus to go back to you and make love to yo thang. She will help you, she know you be comin' ta see her soon."

The next morning Thadeus leaves and Missy goes to Ashanti's house to see her. Ashanti opens the door as if she knew Missy was coming.

"Come on in girl. Um o fix you right up."

There is something in a cup sitting on the table and Ashanti grabs it and says,

"Now you drink that all up and you should be ok after that."

Missy shakes her head and wonders why Ashanti would do something like this for her, knowing how bad she has been to Ashanti. Missy looks at it, then smells the concoction and frowns her face.

"Now, you drink that on down, now. When you go home you get down on your hands and knees and ask Guanab to help you with yo problem."

"Who is Gaunab?"

"Now, don't you worry 'bout that, you just do as I say, if you want to fix yo problem."

Missy drinks the concoction down then hugs Ashanti. As she walks out the door, she turns around and thanks Ashanti again.

Thadeus goes on a river boat and gambles for the first time in his life. He got beginner's luck and wins a lot of money. He and his friends go into a private back room where liquor and prostitutes abound. The prostitutes sit on Thadeus' lap and tease him in between shuffles. He wants to get some white meat, which make him think of what he has at home. He would not touch any of the whores because he is not that type of guy and he has also heard about these women carrying diseases. He gets all riled up by these women which make him horny for his wife.

When he gets home he tries to make advances on Missy. As bad as she wants to, she cannot let him. She has told him that she is on her monthly, so she cannot oblige him. "In fact," Thadeus tells Missy, "I will sleep in one of the guest rooms cuz' I don't feel comfortable sleeping with you like this." He is a little upset and drunk, so he goes right to sleep.

Missy has been praying to Gaunab every night before going to bed. On the morning after the third night, she wakes up and her bed sheets are bloody. She is lucky because Thadeus stayed with Ashanti on this night. She wraps what was in the bed sheet in a towel, then puts paper around it. Geechee knows about it, because she came up stairs to wash the bed sheets. Missy takes the small fetus and buries it behind Ashanti's house. She says a little prayer after it is buried.

She walks around to the front of the house and goes upstairs. The door opens before she could even knock.

"It's gone Baby Girl."

"My name not be Baby Girl, my name be Ashanti."

"Ok, Ashanti."

"And I know it happened," says Ashanti as Missy follows her down the stairs, pointing at the sky where there is a rainbow that goes right down the center of the plantation.

"That's how I know."

Ashanti and Missy become good friends.

Chapter XIV

Missy looks up to Ashanti as a big sister and Ashanti treats her like a little sister. Years have passed and Missy began having children and Ashanti's children began having children. Missy's two daughters are 7 and 8 years of age. They both have thin frames and blond hair and blue eyes. The older of the two is named Machelle and the younger one is Denise. Missy and her two daughters cannot stay away from Ashanti and her grandchildren. They sit on the porch just like the rest of the children listening to Ashanti telling the stories about her home land. One day, while in the mansion, Thadeus is getting ready to go on an evening gambling campaign. The sun is getting ready to set as Thadeus is putting on his necktie in the hall while standing in front of a large mirror. Missy comes behind him and hugs him as he puts on his tie. They are very close and Missy, now understands Thadeus and his ways. She knows how to be happy with what she has. Their two daughters run by, one chasing after the other yelling, "Gaunab gonna get you."

Thadeus finishes tying his tie and turns around looking down at Missy's pretty blue eyes. Her face has a perplexed look on it as she opens her mouth and says, "Thadeus, what is Ganoid?" Thadeus kind of rolls his eyes and replies back, "Don't pay none of that no mind. That just some of dat African hoodoo shit Baby Girl is telling dem chaps." He kisses Missy on the forehead and turns around heading out the door still talking. "I done told that girl bout talkin' 'bout that hoodoo shit. Decent white folks come 'round my chaps thinking they're heathens. That gal needs to stop it!" Little does Thadeus know that Missy is playing it off like she does not know. She knows who Gaunab is.

As the front screen door sways behind Thadeus he sees his three daughters walking by. Two of them are by Missy and the other daughter is by Ashanti who is their Nanny. Missy and some of Ashanti's Daughters gave birth around the same time. They all often play together when chores are done. One of Thadeus's children Wilburt, whom they now call "Uncle Shoe," because he puts horse shoes on horses. He already knows his craft and assists his big brother Thad. Sam is an old man that can still direct young men but can't do much at his old age. Ashanti has also gotten older and now directs most of the work that needs to be done from her house. She is sitting on the porch humming her favorite spiritual, "Wade in the water, wade in the water, children", when Thad junior walks up.

"Mama, now you know you can't be tendin to no chaps in yo spare time. Where dey mamas be?"

"Now you leave these chaps be, if I want to watch them, I will."

"Mama, I come here to get somethin' for Sam's cough."

"Do you know every part of the job you do with Sam?"

"Of course, I've picked up a few of my own tricks on the job. There are thangs he do that are old fashion and he is just stuck in his old ways."

"Well, you give this to old Sam for his cough."

Thad brings the concoction to Sam and he drinks it right down. Next morning Thad comes to the livery stable to start work. Even though Sam is old, he is always up at the break of dawn. Thad goes to the mansion to get Thadeus and Mama up and they all go to Sam's little room in the back of the livery stable. Ashanti bends down to listen to his heart beat but he doesn't have one. "He is as dead as a door knob." Thadeus says.

"Dam, he died in his sleep like one of the animals that Baby Girl gives her medicine to so they can die peacefully."

Ashanti says, "My grand babies might be up, so I best be on my way." She smiles as she turns around now knowing that Sam is indeed dead. As Ashanti works and tends to her children she will often hum "Wade in the water, wade in the water, children".

Thadeus is now a gambler; the more money he makes, the more he gambles. Thadeus bets on cock fights, horse races, craps and poker. Thadeus has become just a gambling man.

BillyRay, is Thadeus' favorite grandchild. He goes everywhere Thadeus goes. BillyRay doesn't do much field work or work at all, for that matter. BillyRay is Thadeus' pet. All of his cousins are mad at him because they have to work the fields while he goes with Masta. He is short with a round head and gets a silly look on his face whenever he is surprised or unsure about something. He squints his eyes and pokes out his lips when this happens. They take river boat rides and go to race tracks and bet on cock fights. They gamble in mansions as well as back woods juke joints and honkey tonks. BillyRay just loves going with Masta. One day BillyRay sees an old man coming through the gates, riding in one of the finest carriages money can buy. "He is the Colonel, who has one of the largest, richest plantations in the state of Mississippi. He has heard tell of Masta's plantation; how grand it is, and wants to see it for himself. Masta gives the Colonel a grand tour of his plantation. Granny Ashanti is wondering, *Who is dis man, and why is he so special, that Thadeus is giving him such a grand tour?* She started walking towards the mansion cuz' Granny knows that the tour will end there over a drink of whiskey or bourbon.

"The Colonel is a tall man with broad shoulders. He has a white beard that goes down his chin, ending in a point. His mustache curls up into a handle bar at both ends. He has a white cowboy hat with a white suit. He was about ten years older than Masta, and you can tell he was a mountain of a man in his day. Masta was not as old as he, even though the years are starting to show on him. Thadeus is definitely in his senior years," states BillyRay.

"Before this tour I had heard a lot 'bout yo Plantation," says the Colonel. "That you had a phenomenal slave girl taking care of everything, making you money hand ova fist."

"Yea, Baby Girl is quite a gal." Ashanti kind of smiles as they both give her accolades.

"Well, I hope you put them in their place."

"What do you mean, Colonel?"

"I mean that they are on the level just before you get to an animal. We are far more superior than them. That's why God put us ova them, to rule them and keep them in their place. I don't care how much money mine make me, I always let them know that they ain't nothing but animals. Every now and then you must tell them that to keep them in their place."

Ashanti hears everything both of them said. After they finish their drinks the Colonel says, "Thanks for the tour, the drink and yo company. I must be off. Now you keep up the good work 'round here and maybe one day your spread can be as big as mine."

Geechee hands the Colonel his hat as Thadeus walks him to the door.

At that moment Ashanti comes around the corner, "Now Thadeus, I know you ain't listening to that foolishness that old man talkin' 'bout." "Now, watcho mouth, you don't talk about no white man that way. Stay in yo place! You are just above those animals you sire, that's why you get along with them so well. We are superior ova y'all!"

"If y'all be so superior ova us, then why do y'all need us to do the work and most of the thinkin'? I go into town and talk to some of the other captives and most of them say the same thing; that y'all don't know what y'all doin'. We bought the knowledge from our home land to help y'all do things that y'all knew nothing about and y'all get the credit fo' it."

"Now Girl I done heard enough. You goan bout yo business cuz' I done heard enough from you." Thadeus yells out as she is leaving, "Now you go take yo old black ass somewhere and get some work done!"

Thadeus follows her to the back door of the mansion still ranting and raving. Ashanti turns around after getting her wits back and says. "Thadeus since yo ass done got old and gray all you do is drink and gamble. You don't even know what be going on, on yo own plantation. Thadeus yells back at Ashanti's last response. "Yo sex use ta be good, you old hag now it ain't worth nothin. I don't even come 'round yo old stanken ass no mo'."

"I got a white wife who is prettier than you and younger than you." "You old man, you can't even get it up and when yo wife thinks about good lovin' she ain't thinkin' 'bout you. I be the one who made you; I be the one who give you luck when you be out there gamblin. It be all done now! You need to keep our, I mean, my grandson home fo' he get into some trouble running behind you witcho lazy gambling ass!"

"Ok girl, you done said enough. You betta goan befo' I take a lashin' ta ya's! You better stop running off at the mouth if ya know whats good furr ya. You got to stay in yo place." The days of a superior plantation and luck with his gambling are now over. Ashanti does not have to put a Mojo on the plantation for it to fail, she just has to let go of her will and focus for all good things to come to an end.

A week later Thadeus' luck starts to change. He begins to lose night after night. BillyRay pleads with him to quit but he will not do so. He looks over at BillyRay and says, "Now, don't you tell yo Granny nothing 'bout me losing'. Ya hear me boy?" BillyRay looks over at Thadeus with the characteristically silly look on his face and nods his head yes.

Thadeus sees Ashanti a couple weeks later and yells down to her, "You old hag, you ain't got nothin to do wit' me winning cuz' I won a shit load of money last night!"

"Don't worry, sometimes my venom works slowly. Don't you even worry."

The cows' milk becomes sour, livestock began miscarrying, and people have stopped coming by to be healed by Ashanti. Ashanti just looks out her window and sees the demise that is happening before her eyes. Thadeus keeps acting like everything is ok as he continues to gamble, neglecting his family, his farm and himself. He incrementally starts dressing bummy and his clothes are not neatly pressed; nails are not manicured and hair is not combed.

That next evening BillyRay and Thadeus go and gamble on this big river boat. They walk up a gang plank that leads to the front door. They sit down and Thadeus starts playing poker. BillyRay notices that the men are cheating by passing cards to each other. When Thadeus was backed by Ashanti, Thadeus used to beat the socks off these men playing poker even when they cheated. BillyRay tries to alert Thadeus but he won't listen. Thadeus ends up losing four of his slaves behind this card game. BillyRay says to the Thadeus,

"I tried to tell you what dem men be doing."

"Ah shut up boy you too late for all that now." Thadeus continues to think to himself, "How am I going to tell that old hag that I will have to give up one or two of her grand's." His heart is heavy because he has to do what he has to do. The next morning he tells one of his chaps to go get Granny because this is what she is called now. Ashanti wonders what Thadeus wants. She begins to ponder. *I wonder if he is going to apologize, I wonder if he wants to make love to me again.* As she is saying this she is washing up. As she contemplates making love to Thadeus again she squirts some perfume on her private area. Ashanti walks into Thadeus' room stopping just in front of him. She puts her hands behind her with her head down low enough where she can look up at him submissively. "Thadeus you be wanting me?" Thadeus is hesitant about telling her, so he musters up the nerve to tell her. "Yea well two of yo I mean our grand's got to be sold." "Yo dumb lazy ass done lost my chaps gamblin'. You betta sell yo own." Thadeus becomes enraged from what came out of Ashanti's mouth. Thadeus slaps Ashanti to the floor with all his might. Ashanti hits the ground and rolls over on her belly facing Thadeus. "I don't allow no niggras to sass me." Ashanti stumbles to her feet still dazed wiping blood out the corner of her mouth. She gives Thadeus the look of death. Thadeus turns away from her piercing big brown eyes waving his hands to shoo her away. "You go on about yo business cuz' I done told you too many times about yoself."

Ashanti turns and walks away hurt from what just happened. She then gets a smirk of death on her face; Ashanti leaves the house heartbroken as a tear falls down her face.

She knows she has to work another Mojo. The next morning Ashanti goes to the mansion while Bulla is cooking Thadeus's and Missy's breakfast. Ashanti nudges Bulla away from the stove. Bulla looks back at Ashanti as if to say, "What you doing." Ashanti gives Bulla a look that made her back away from the stove. Ashanti sprinkles some ingredients from her pouch in his eggs. She put his food on a tray with a glass of orange juice and slowly and majestically starts walking up the spiraling stair case to give Thadeus his food. As she is walking she begins to chant, ending it with a hoarse voiced Zooka Mallie. When she opens the door Missy and Thadeus are lying in the bed. Missy says MMM breakfast." Ashanti looks at her and Missy quickly changes her tune. "I'll just leave y'all be and have them whip me up some breakfast." Missy walks out the door heading to the kitchen. Ashanti says nothing, she just fluffs the pillows behind Thadeus as he sits up. She places the tray over his lap and Thadeus begins to eat. Ashanti stands there not saying anything as Thadeus start gobbling up the food. He then says with food in his mouth "Now Baby Girl I did not mean to hit you but you kept on running off at the mouth. Aint no niggra suppose to talk to no white man like that." Ashanti's heart sinks in her chest hoping that Thadeus would have apologized instead of saying what he just said. She humbly backed away semi curtseying, listening to the foolishness that did not apply to the success of the plantation. When she is out of sight her body becomes rigid and a diabolical smile appears on her face,

It is early in tthe morning when the rooster begins to crow. Something about this morning does not seem right. BillyRay notes, *Master is never up dis time of monin,' he is usually still in bed. This monin' he knocks on everyone's door tellin them to get up and get dressed. He tells everyone to meet him in the north pasture. The day befo, Masta's brother came and got most of the men to help him on his plantation.*

Masta would do this from time to time to help his brother Douglas. These men are lucky not to be on the plantation on this day. Something told me not to go with Masta, so I didn't go. I hid in the woods to see what be goin on.

Masta got a look on his face that I ain't ever seen befo. Masta shouts out for everyone to start diggin. So everyone began diggin a deep, long ditch. Masta has a look on his face, as if someone was controllin his every move. He has the look of two faces. His clothes are mangled and not put on with much care. His face needs a shave and his teeth look like he just ate some raw meat.

The hole was plenty deep and long. Masta had the rest of my brothers, sisters, aunts and uncles to get inta the hole. Granny stands at the top of the hole with her arms crossed as if she did not have to go. He points the shot gun at her to let her know that he means business. One of my uncles helpes Granny down into the hole. I see the look on everyone's face. They have nothin but fear in their eyes. The children are cryin and movin 'round in the hole. Masta began shootin them one by one. He has hand guns in all of his pockets. When one is finished he quickly pulls out another one and begins shooting again. Before he could shoot Granny, she shouts some words in her old African language, "Zooka Mallie!" then, Masta shoots her right between her eyes.

After everyone was killed he himself began burying them, slamming his foot down on the shovel as hard as he could to get big clumps of dirt to throw on them. He has this very sick look on his face, like he has someone inside of him. I did not know what I was going to do. I remember Granny always tellin me to follow the North Star, that it would take me to freedom. Now, all my family murdered by Masta, I have no one. I decide to gather some food and wait for midnight to start my journey. So I went back to the shack and hid under my bed until nightfall where I fell asleep."

Chapter XV

BillyRay gets awakened by some clumping sounds on the wooden floor. It sounds like the hooves of horses and the rattling of chains. *So I lay silent because I think that it is Masta. I begin to hear the sweet sound of grandma's humming. 'Wade in the water, wade in the water, children.' I slowly push my head from underneath the bed, just to see Granny's head looking out the door. I slid out from underneath the bed and ran over to granny. What I see stops me in my tracks. Granny's head was on the body of a mule. When Granny turns her head toward me her eyes were white and had no color. Her skin is dark and ashey and she also has sharp teeth like a bear. Her hair is corn rolled which turns into a mane as they go down her neck.* She whispers to me, Follow the North Star, it will take you to freedom.'

"But granny!"

"Hush boy, I don't want you to wake yo Masta; I got business to take care of at the big house when the moon is full.

Billy runs by her looking up at the sky. The moon is full but it is covered by drifting clouds. "Even though Masta got the two faces and he killed my whole family, I must warn him that Granny's comin. Great day! Granny's a haint! I thought Haints are here to protect us. This Haint has fire in her eyes. I think it will kill Masta and his family. I must warn him."

BillyRay runs as fast as he can to the mansion. He begins knocking on the back door of the kitchen, "Let me in, let me in!" No one answers, so he slowly creeps through the door. He notices that MayBell, Bulla and Geechee are nowhere to be seen. "I guess Masta musta killed dem too."

BillyRay tip toes through the kitchen into the dining room where he sees Master's wife and his children standing over him. Master lies on the floor with blood streaming from his head. In and around the pool of blood glass is splattered everywhere.

"Missy," BillyRay says. Missy looks back at BillyRay. "Thadeus was acting crazy, he was trying to take the girls outside so I broke the vase over his head."

"Missy," interrupts Billy, "What I am going to tell you will be hard fo you to believe. Masta killed my whole family. He made them dig a hole then he had them get down in it and shot them all. Granny was the last one he shot. She said some words from her home land, "Zooka Mallie," while holding the pouch she always wears 'round her neck, before he shot her between the eyes. When I left he was burying them. It was a good thang that Douglas needed most of my family for his plantation or they would have all got killed. Some of the children, elderly and grown folks stayed behind and got shot by masta.

You know Missy, Granny use' ta work magic, she got it from Africa. Granny is coming here to kill alla y'all."

"Now BillyRay, stop talking that foolishness, if Granny's dead, she's dead."

"No Missy, Granny's a Haint. I saw her! Granny's head is on the body of a mule. She has teeth like a bear and her eyes are dingy white as dusty picked cotton. She has foul smelling green stuff oozing out the bullet hole in her forehead. I tell you Missy she out to get y'all."

The sound of hooves clipity, clack, clipity, clack are heard outside the kitchen door. The door begins to slowly open as it makes a long creaking sound. BillyRay jumps in front of Missy, Master, and their two daughters in order to protect them from what is about to come. BillyRay shouts, "Granny, I can't let you hurt Masta and his chaps. Two wrongs don't make no right. I thought Haints are suppose to protect, not to do hurt."

The sound of hooves gets closer. The banging of pans and the nudging of chairs make it apparent that something is on its way. BillyRay shouts, "Now Granny, I know you hear me, I can't let you hurt masta's family. Now, turn around and go back to where you came from!"

Granny's head appears around the corner first. Her eyes are a dingy white color, like freshly picked cotton. Her pointed teeth hang out her mouth dripping saliva. The foul smelling green fluid is dripping out the bullet hole that is in between her eyes. Her skin is very dingy and dirty looking. The rest of her body follows. It is the body of a mule with a dingy brown coat. She stands in the middle of the living room's floor with the look of death in her eyes. Missy and the two girls cling to BillyRay like a cat that is about to get a bath.

Granny's tail sways back and forth like a cat that is getting ready to pounce on a mouse.

"BillyRay, you ain't got no right protecting dem. Dis between me and Thadeus," says Granny in a deep distorted voice.

"Granny, two wrongs don't make no right. I can't let you do this."

"BillyRay, are you going to risk your life to save the life of someone that killed yo family?"

"Granny, I just can't let you do this, so be gone."

"Seeing that you warned them, I can't work my pain, so I will leave. But remember this, BillyRay, foe generations after next, I will get" Granny takes two steps backwards, then disappears.

Missy and the two girls slowly let go of BillyRay. Their faces are still full of fear. Missy looks into BillyRay's eyes with fear and curiosity.

"BillyRay, what did Granny mean by foe generations after next, I will get?"

BillyRay slides down against the wall until he is fully seated on the floor with a bewildered look on his face, and replies, "Missy, I don't right know, I knows it ain't no good a comin'."

BillyRay falls asleep on the dining room's floor, which is never heard of in those times. House slaves, in fact, no slave are allowed to lounge nowhere in their master's house. They have designated places where they go to sleep.

BillyRay gets awakened by a couple of nudges on his shoulder. He quickly jumps up as if he was ready to run. "BillyRay, BillyRay, wake up, wake up." To BillyRay's surprise it is his uncle "Shoe." He is called that because he puts horse shoes on all the work animals.

"Uncle Shoe, Uncle Shoe, you're alive."

"Yes BillyRay. I hid when I saw Masta get his shot gun, having that twisted look on his face."

Uncle shoe is a short, stocky, brown skinned man. He has broad shoulders and large rough looking hands.

"What got inta Masta? Uncle Shoe."

"Well, BillyRay, as you know, Masta loves to gamble."

"He was a good gambler," replies BillyRay.

"Yea, but those guys down at that river boat love to cheat."

"I told Masta we need to stop going down there 'cause I seen them passing cards. Masta did not want to listen, he keep a goin' down there anyways, thinkin' he gonna win his money back."

"Well, anyways, BillyRay, he lost a lot of money and he bet two of my brothers and lost." "I know I know I was there when it happened."

"I overheard him talkin' to Mama 'bout what he had to do. Sellin' two of her chaps ova gamblin' did not sit too well with Mama, so Mama told him that he was not goan do nothin' like that. He slap Mama to the ground, tellin' her he did not 'llow no niggras to sass him or tell him what ta do. I was standin' unda' his winda' goin' ta yell up ta him what I need when he go back ta town." Thadeus allows him to do this because he is Ashanti and Thadeus's son. "You know all Mama's chaps is his. So Ma, who was raised by a village witch docta, worked a hoodoo on Masta." "Yea Uncle Shoe, I know Granny spoke a lot about her home land. I remember when the sky got dark she would run around yellin' "everyone get in, cuz' Shangó a comin'," most of the chaps would gatha' 'round her in her house and listen to her tell stories about her home land. Only she would be talkin' we had to be quiet and bees our behinds still."

"She'an did us the same way when we were little chaps," says Uncle Shoe. "She would tell us Obatalá made us and no one should own another. Then she would sing to us 'Wade in the wadah', and 'Follow the North Star'."

"She would also teach the girls about what's in the wild, so they could use it to cook and do healin' with. She would also tell us that nothing is greater than us in de whole universe. As he is saying this him and BillyRay would stare into the sky.

BillyRay looks up with a smile and says, "I use' to love how she would smile and jump around after seeing a rainbow in the sky."

"I know all that BillyRay cuz' she raised me too.

"Well, any ways, gettin' back to what I was talkin' 'bout. The next monin' after being smacked to the floor, Granny is up very early. She leaves her home and goes to the mansion. The women were in the kitchen cooking breakfast. Granny told Bulla that she would finish Thadeus' breakfast and bring it to him. Bulla did not wanna do it and looked at Granny, not wanting to hand over skillet. Granny gave her a hard look and Bulla handed her the duty of fixin' Thadeus' breakfast. Thadeus was waitin' in his room for his breakfast. Granny took the pouch from around her neck and began pouring the stuff be in her pouch inta Thadeus' grits and eggs. Then she say somethin' in her old language. She brought the food up to his room where Thadeus was waitin'. When Granny came into the room, Thadeus was shocked to see her.

Thadeus said, "I didn't mean to slap ya. I have to take care of my own business." Granny smiles and hands Thadeus his food. After giving him his food she bowed, walkin' backward with a silly grin on her face. Thadeus start gobblin' up he food. The Mojo Ashanti worked by puttin' it in his food was suppose ta kill he own family, but it work backwards, because he wanted to kill everyone. It was a good thang that most of our kin' went to work over at Douglas's place or they woulda met the same thang the uddens."

"Uncle Shoe, I thought haints suppose' to protect you."

"Well, BillyRay, you protected Masta family from Mama and her goan get you and yo'ns. You better find out how to stop her 'cause she dam show comin' back. Whatever you learn', you'n better pass it down to yo kin' fo' years to come."

BillyRay and Uncle Shoe sit on the steps of the mansion not knowing what's going to happen next. They both look into the sky with wonder and curiosity, as a rainbow appears.

That was no regular morning on the Wellington plantation. What happened that day and the night before, would affect the inhabitants of this southern plantation for years to come. The animals would need tending to as well as the fields. There is no sound of laughter from children playing. BillyRay and Uncle Shoe sit on the stoop of the plantation house with worried looks on their faces not knowing what has been unleashed. It is the coming of the Haint!

Chapter XVI

The year is 2005 in this southern Mississippi rural town called Bogue Chitto. A black man and a seventeen year old white boy are about to cross each other's path. They meet at an old dirt road down the street from the Wellington Trailer Park. The boy yells out,

"Nigga! What you doin' 'round these parts?"

"You know who I am?" replies the man. "I'm RayPaul. I been knowing yo family since I was knee high to a puppy. BillyRay, me and yo uncle went to school together."

"I don't give a dam who you know; y'all people ain't suppose to be 'round these parts."

As BillyRay is talking RayPaul begins squinting his eyes and poking his lips out.

"BillyRay, I come to warn you, she back, she back for blood."

"What the hell you talkin' bout, nigga?"

"Granny came back to get us; she got fire in her eyes."

As they speak, they both smell a foul odor and hear the sound of rattling chains followed by the sweet sound of humming, "Wade in the water, wade in the water, children". The humming is soothing and sounds like an angel catching the spirit; the smell is a combination of rotten eggs and burnt sulfur from a match. RayPaul's eyes widen with fear and sweat begins to pour all over his face. He looks at BillyRay and yells out, "You better run, she's here!"

Even though BillyRay hears the humming and smells the foul odor, he did not believe RayPaul, yet and still he feels his fear and they both take off in opposite directions. BillyRay runs into the trailer park where he lives and RayPaul runs into the woods at the end of the trailer park. As RayPaul runs through the woods of the old Wellington estate he suddenly hears the sound of galloping hooves. As he is running, he is yells out, "Granny, I am yo kin, why you want to harm me?"

RayPaul falls to the ground after stumbling over a root of a tree. He feels something standing over him. He slowly turns over onto his back and sees these large white eyes that are glowing in the moon light. He is face to face with Granny. Saliva begins to drip onto his face from Granny's sharp fangs. Her head is on the body of a mule.

"Granny, why you gonna kill me? um yo kin"

She speaks out in a deep raspy voice, "You are BillyRay's fourth generation. I am here to do something I was suppose to do a long time ago, but your great granddaddy stopped me. You were over there trying to warn them and do what your great great granddaddy did. Um glad you came to the plantation. Now, a Granny's got to do what a Granny's got to do."

Granny begins to kick and stomp RayPaul. All that can be heard is his bones cracking, the thudding of hooves and the ripping of flesh with her sharp teeth. When she finishes, she looks down at the mangled body and says. "One down, and mo' ta go!" Granny grabs the mangled flesh by his clothes and begins to drag him out the woods and across the old dirt road to a patch of woods that sits between the highway and the trailer park. Granny wants the Wellington family to see what is coming to them.

A couple days after the carnage, workers from a chain gang are cleaning and cutting bushes along a small stretch of highway which spends little time in this small town. One of the worker's face frowns because he has discovered a smell that is unbearable. He looks around to see where it is coming from. He sees a frenzy of flies hovering over what he thinks is road kill. Knowing that he was going to have to clean it up, he creeps over to see what unlucky animal didn't make it across the highway. He parts the grass just to come to the shocking view of a badly mutilated human body. He jumps back to get this scene out of his sight. He runs as fast as he can to the foreman, who is on horseback overseeing the work detail. The foreman is a tall stocky man with one hand on the reins and the other holding his shot gun in the air with its butt resting on his thigh.

"Mista, mista, there is a badly hacked up human body over yonder in the grass."

"Boy that ain't no human body, that some dam deer or coon."

"No, no, mista; ain't no deer got tennis shoes on!"

"Let me go over there and see for myself!"

He pulls on the reins to turn the horse around and he heads toward the spot the inmate pointed to. The horse starts swinging its tail back and forth to swat flies as it trots in that direction. The closer the horse gets to the spot where the body is, the more reluctant it acts. The horse begins to buck and starts trotting sideways until it comes to a complete stop and would not go any farther. The foreman has to dismount and walk the rest of the way.

As he leans over, he parts the grass with the hand that is holding the shot gun while the other hand covers his mouth and nose because of the unbearable stench. It is the remains of a badly mutilated human body. He jumps back and grabs his radio and calls the sheriff to come over and investigate.

The dispatcher calls out, "There is a possible homicide on 51, near the Wellington Trailer Park." Two officers are nearby and one of them responds to the call. He picks up the radio and speaks, "This is car 60, we are in the area and we are headed that way." He then asks his police partner, "Douglas, ain't that over by your brother's trailer park?"

"Yes indeed, Bady."

"It's probably some of that trash from that trailer park that's dead. "Now yo brother really ain't going to get his rent's money. He chuckles as he is speaking. Douglas your sister and yo nephew still live there?"

"Yes indeed, they still do."

"That good for nothin, pot lickin' husband still with her?"

"Sho is."

As the car gets closer to the crime scene, something seems to bother Douglas.

"Dam Bady, I got this chill that's running all through my body."

The two officers stop directly in front of the crime scene. Bady gets out the car first repositioning his Billy Club and adjusting his gun in his holster. Douglas reluctantly slides out of the police car and heads toward the body. They both cover their mouths and noses almost at the same time as they slowly part the grass to look at the victim.

The body is badly mangled and flesh is ripped away from bone. The head is completely smashed in and all its bones seem like they are broken. As the two men back away Bady says, "Dam Douglas, what the hell got hold of that? They were not intendin' for it to live."

"Bady, you got me on this one cuz' I ain't never seen nuttin' like that befo in all my days. The only thing I know is that the victim is definitely a darky cuz' I can tell by the nappy hair."

As they peer around the body they notice hoof prints everywhere.

"Douglas, these look like hoof prints all 'round the body."

"Bady, look at his head, it looks like a hoof print right in the center of his face. The lower forehead, eyes, and nose are smashed into the victims' skull. If there was not any hair on the victim's head you would not know what part of the body it was. Ain't that Ol' Al Tuggle on that horse yonder?"

"Yea Bady, that's Old Al."

"You think these are the hoof prints of Ol' Al's horse, look at them, they are all 'round the body. Let's go over and ask Ol' Al." Al is about 50 feet away from them overseeing the work detail.

Al begins loading the inmates back on the bus, "Hurry up, y'all load up, on the bus. Y'all ain't done a dam thang all day, just standin' 'round bein' nosey."

Bady and Douglas walk up to Al, who is still sitting on his horse.

"What ya say dair?" Douglas asks Al as he reaches out his hand to shake Al's, and Bady does the same.

"Douglas, asks Al, "Did you come close to the body with your horse? cuz' we seen a lot of hoof prints all over in and around the body."

"No Douglas, my horse would not even go close, he kinda bucked me if I would have kept tryin' to make him get closer. I had to walk over to see the body."

"Terrible thang now, ain't it? I ain't ever seen nothin' like that befo'," states Bady.

The two officers shake Al's hand before walking away. As they walk back to the car Douglas tells Bady, "I think we are going to have to call Jackson for one of those top notched investigators to come down here and investigate." "Douglas, we will probably need a zoologist cuz' this looks like a animal attack. Horses and mules don't kill people, unless they are ordered to do so," replies Bady. "Bady, we ain't no experts at this. We will let those big shot investigators from Jackson figure this one out."

As they walk back to their car, two other officers begin taping off the crime scene, the stench and the flies. "Bady, something just ain't right, that crime scene feels to me as though I am somehow connected to it." Douglas is the second oldest of the four Wellington children. He is a deputy at the Brookhaven Police Department. He is about 5'10 with blond hair and blue eyes. He has a muscular body which shows through his sheriff's uniform. He is also a college grad who sometime regresses into using that old southern slang. He is intelligent and very articulate. He is single and does not have any children. He is a descendent of Thadeus Wellington.

"Douglas, your great, great, great, great grandfather owned the property not even 100 yards away from the crime scene. That land's been in y'alls family for a long time. When it reached y'alls generation you guys turned part of it into a trailer park."

"Bady, you might as well say it's my brother's because I don't get a dam dime of that money."

Bady, with a bewildered look on his face says, "Maybe you are right, I don't think anything like that should be happening around your family's property." Something just ain't right,"

Douglas replies, "I can't quite put my finger on it." Bady is a little taller than Douglas with black hair. His back slumps when he walks and he has poor posture. He always has a carefree look on his face. His uniform is clean, but not neatly ironed. He is just another one of those "good old boys."

The police car pulls down the old country road leaving clouds of dust. The death in front of the Wellington Trailer Park is the beginning of the fulfillment of a prophecy. They pull up in front of the police station that looks like it was left over from an old western movie set. As the two men walk through the door EmmaLiz the dispatcher smiles at Douglas and Bady while saying, "What's good?" As she pops her gum and peers at them looking over the top of her glasses. The ceiling is full of fans that are moving at high speeds as well as the sound of air conditioners trying to ward off that Mississippi heat. She is a skinny African America woman with long brown hair that she keeps in a bun. Her skin is very dark and shiny as though she polishes herself before coming to work. She loves gossip and tries to get as much as she can from the officers. As the two men pass EmmaLiz, they wave their hands at her as if to say 'not now.' She smirks and looks back at one of the computer screens on her desk.

After being propositioned by EmmaLiz they stop and let Old Blue, the station's mascot, sniff them as he wags his tail. This seems to be the ritual the men go through every time they initially enter the police station for the day. Bady looks over at Douglas and says, "Douglas, was it a full moon out last night? Do you think that had something to do with the murder?"

"Yea Bady, it was one of dem werewolves that did it. Let's just tell Sheriff Bodine what we saw and file our report."

The sheriff is sitting in his office with a cigar in the corner of his mouth reading the funnies in the newspaper. He has brown stains around the rim of his lips because he also chews tobacco. He is a short, potbellied man that wears his sheriff's hat with pride. He also waddles when he walks. Douglas clears his throat to respectfully interrupt the sheriff from entertaining himself. Bady stops just before the entrance of the sheriff's door. Bady is a little intimidated by the sheriff, so he lets Douglas carry on with the interruption.

"Excuse me sheriff," says Douglas. The sheriff takes the cigar out of his mouth, slamming the paper down on top of his desk,

"This better be impotant, to disturb me while I'm readin."

"Well sheriff, there was a murder not even 50 yards in front of the trailer park."

"Maybe your brother kill 'em for not paying rent at that rat trap y'all call a trailer park." The sheriff laughs as he is making this statement.

"You should have seen how badly the body was mutilated," continues Douglas. "Sheriff, it was beat up so bad that if it did not have any clothing on, you could not tell if it was human or animal."

Bady comes to the entrance of the sheriff's office to see what is going on.

"We are going to call Jackson to get an investigator down here in order to get an I.D. on the body," states Douglas.

"You two leave that to me," interrupts the sheriff, "I'll take care of that my dam self. So you guys scoot; go on somewhere and do some police work."

The two officers waddle out of the office like two scolded children.

"Listen Bady, I am going to roll over to my brother's to see if he knows what happened and what his gut feeling is."

"Douglas, you going to his house?"

"No, he ain't at his house this time of day; he is on the riverboat gambling. I would bet a week's pay on it."

The two officers drive over to the river boat which is lit up like a Christmas tree. Over the front of the entrance is a large sign lit up with bright lights that reads "Old Dixie Casino." The river boat has very large paddles in the back of it to propel it through the water. It is designed like the old river boats used during the time of the Civil War. It is in a river that is dark and murky. There is a long and wide gang plank that connects the land to the entrance of it.

The two men walk in the casino through the main door and head over toward the crap tables.

"Bady, my brother loves to shoot dice. I love to do it too but I always lose so I don't play much."

Bady sees Douglases brother and points at him. The officers' pace quickens as they walk towards him. Thadeus happens to look up and sees them coming his way. The two officers slow down and gingerly step to Thadeus's side of the table. They are acting as though they are approaching royalty.

"This better be important because I done lost a lot of money," says Thadeus as he shifts the dice in his hand, ready to release them onto the table.

"Well, uh, there was a murder in front of the trailer park."

"So why are you tellin' me?"

"Well, uh, we wanted to know if you noticed anything unusual going on."

"Douglas, you know I don't go no where 'round that place. I don't even like going there to get my rent money. I don't have no idea what happened there last night. All right, y'all two scat, I got to win some of my money back. Call me later 'cause it did happen in front of my place, so I need to know what's going on."

Thadeus is the oldest of the Wellingtons. He is about six foot tall and is built well for a man in his late forties. He has blond hair and blue eyes. He loves to gamble on anything. He is a very successful business man and owns a mansion on the other side of the trailer park. He earns most of his money from the stock market.

The two officer's walk back to their car not knowing where they are going or what they are going to do next.

Chapter XVII

A cell phone rings and someone hesitantly answers. "Hello, what can I help you with?" The individual pauses in anticipation of what is going to be said.

"Listen little sis, I did not put you in your predicament. Mama and daddy gave you the best. You went to the best schools, wore the best clothes and had the best upbringing anyone could have. Hell you went to private schools while the rest of us went to public schools. You chose this life style."

He pauses again, waiting for a reply from the person on the other side.

"I will get him out of there, or my name ain't Thadeus Wellington the fourth."

The person he is talking to, is his baby sister RoseMary. She has been complaining about her husband. Thadeus slams the lid of his phone while walking out the casino in an aggravated manner. The Wellington Trailer Park is a rundown, low income, poverty stricken residential area. Most of the people who live there have lost all hope in their lives, one of which is the baby sister of the Wellington family, RoseMary. There are four members of the Wellington Klan. Thadeus is the oldest followed by Douglas and Robert who resides in Chicago. RoseMary is short with blond hair and blue eyes. She has pretty dimples when she smiles, which accents her pretty white teeth and her full juicy lips. Her waist is small and her hips are wide which gives her an hour glass figure. She has a seventeen year old son named BillyRay Wellington. He kept her last name because, his father took off on her before he was born and he was not married to her. She is married to an unemployed, womanizing husband named Glenn. She steps out of her trailer wiping the sweat off her forehead caused by the mid-day hot Mississippi heat. She puts her hand over her eyebrows to block the glare of the sun as she canvases the area.

She then hollers out, "BillyRay, BillyRay, where are you?" A dirty faced boy appears from around the corner of the trailer.

"Yea ma', what do you want? "

"Don't you 'what ma' me!" replies RoseMary.

"You need to clean up after yourself I ain't yow maid."

"Then, what are you?"

RoseMary swats at BillyRay to shoo him into the trailer. BillyRay has long brown hair that drops just above his shoulders. He also has light brown eyes and a wise guy look on his face. BillyRay is about 5'11 with a medium build. He seems to want to dress and act like Glenn, his stepfather.

A beat up old pickup truck pulls up in front of the trailer. A man gets out with a dirty ripped up T shirt and jeans with grease marks on his thighs, as though he has been wiping his hands in the same spot for months. RoseMary Yells out, "Glenn, I hope you got a job because I told you not to come back unless you had one."

"Well baby, I have an interview in the monin."

"Having an interview don't mean you have a job."

He eases up toward her and wraps his arms around her waist as he speaks. There are three steps that lead up to the landing, which is surrounded by rails, before you get to the front door. RoseMary is standing on the landing, leaning on the rail, while she is talking to Glenn. As he wraps his arms around her he whispers in her ear. The seriousness in her voice softens as his words seduce her once again. As he eases her inside the door, nibbling on her neck and talking softly in her ear; they both disappear behind the slam of a squeaky trailer door. Glenn is not much taller than RoseMary. He has brown hair which he wears down to his shoulder with light brown eyes. He looks like a cross between a rock star and a cowboy since he always wears a cowboy hat. He is a real ladies' man.

Meanwhile the two deputies are in their car trying to figure out what happened.

"Bady, I still think I am somehow connected to what happened over there. I want to go pay a visit to my sister and nephew and see if they know anything."

Thadeus pulls up before Bady and Douglas do. Thadeus is upset because his baby sister's good for nothing husband is still living with her. Basically he is just living off her and doing nothing for himself or his family. BillyRay likes

Glenn because he usually takes BillyRay with him to get drunk and play video games. Glenn also talks about how he won his belt buckle in the prison rodeo, as well as other prison stories, which fascinates BillyRay.

"I ain't giving her no mo money to take care of that bum!" shouts Thadeus talking to himself out loud. He slams on his brekes when he reaches his sister's trailer. He quickly jumps out of his car and barges into her trailer. Thadeus does not say a word as he barges past BillyRay and begins throwing Glenn from wall to wall in the tight hall way of the trailer. There is shouting and noise from the two scuffling men doing battle. RoseMary is trying to break up the fight while BillyRay laughs at the spectacle. They stumble out the door and down the few steps off the small porch of the trailer house. They end up rolling around on the ground, doing battle. Thadeus gets the upper hand on Glenn as he rolls on top of him pinning him to the ground. Thadeus then straddles Glenn with his knees, pinning Glenn's arms down where he can't move them as he begins to pound on Glenn's face with his fists. RoseMary shouts, "Stop, stop, you're going to kill him!" as she is trying to pull Thadeus off Glenn, to no avail. A police car pulls up. Bady and Douglas jump out to break up the fight.

"Thadeus, get off of him 'for you kill him!" Screams Douglas.

"I am sick and tired of supporting that skid row bum."

"Big brother, I don't like him much either, but RoseMary has to make her own choices in life"

Finally Thadeus gets off Glenn and Douglas tries to help Glenn up. Glenn snatches his arm away from Douglas, as if he does not want his help. Glenn is dazed from all the blows he took to his head, so he staggers as he gets up. He is bleeding from his mouth and nose. He yells out, "You Wellingtons think you're God's gift to the world. Y'all ain't nothin' but money hungry sons of bitches."

RoseMary yells at Glenn, "Leave, leave and don't come back!"

"Glenn if I was you I would stop talkin' 'bout the Wellingtons, for Thadeus jump back on you." Bady is laughing as he speaks.

Glenn climbs in his truck spinning, his wheels, leaving a cloud of dust. Both brothers hug their little sister to calm her down. Douglas asks his sister if she has heard or knows anything about the murder.

"I went to bed kinda early that night because I was not feeling well. The only thing that struck me odd was a very bad odor I would smell from time to

141

time. It was a smell I had never smelled before."

"Well uncle," says BillyRay, "I was talkin' to that boy, RayPaul, that night 'bout being 'round our parts. We stopped when we heard some humming and chains rattling. Sounded like it was one of them old nigga granny's humming, one of their church songs. It was followed by a very foul smell. It was coming from the bushes next to the end of the trailer park. RayPaul took off one way and I went the other."

"That's funny you said that BillyRay, I been hearing that same humming and chains rattling when that bad smell comes around." interjects RoseMary, "Every time it happens I get a cold feeling all through my body." Douglas begins scratching his head with a bewildered look on his face. Thadeus asks, "Do you think RayPaul had something to do with that murder?"

"We don't know. We were going over there to question RayPaul."

"Big brother, follow me and I will show you what I am talkin' bout," replies Douglas.

When they arrive at the murder scene Thadeus cringes. Douglas has the same feeling. Douglas looks over to Thadeus saying, "You see what I mean?"

"Yea Douglas, I had this cold chill run all through my body. It feels as though I am somehow connected to it. Something just ain't right. I'll talk to you guys later. I'm getting the hell out of here." Thadeus hops in his car and speeds off, not knowing that he has a lot to do with the event that has taken place.

Douglas and Bady leave, on their way to RayPaul's place. The black Wellingtons were given about 100 acres of land on the far end of the plantation shortly after the Civil War. It was the area where the slave quarters were and where the massacre took place. Bady asks, "Douglas, wasn't that land those black Wellingtons are on once y'alls?"

"I believe so. They were given the land shortly after slavery was over."

Douglas laughs, "There's a whole tribe of dem bastards livin' there and they ain't leavin'."

Douglas looks at Bady and shakes his head as Bady continues to laugh. As they pull up to RayPaul's house they notice a lot of moving around in and around his house. There was a truck being loaded with belongings from the house. The family has built houses on lots next to each other, separated by long stretches of empty space. Behind the ten or fifteen houses and trailers there are fields of crops. On the very end of where the crops are grown is a patch of land with a fence and flowers inside the fence neatly placed and a big wooden cross in the middle of it.

Officers Bady and Douglas get out of their car and walk into the house to see what is going on. They walk in the house and see JeanAnn and her children running around grabbing whatever they can, and loading it on a truck. JeanAnn is short with short brown hair puffed out in a small afro. She has full lips that quiver when she pronounces her words. Douglas speaks out, "JeanAnn, where are you going in such a hurry?"

"Mr. Douglas, we ain't stayin 'round here. Hell done opened up and I ain't going."

"JeanAnn, where is your husband?"

"I ain't seen him, but someone told me that was he who was killed near the trailer park."

"JeanAnn, how do you know it's him?"

"He ain't been home in a few days and my sister's son called here and told me that the person they found dead is RayPaul 'cause RayPaul is the only one that keep a quarter in his ear. I'm leaving cuz' she done come back."

Douglas replies, with a bewildered look on his face, "Who come back?"

"Granny Haint, that's who, she done come back for blood."

"What you mean, JeanAnn?"

A couple of JeanAnne's children run by hollering "Guanna goan get chew!"

"You should know Mista Douglas, y'all peoples involved in it too.

RayPaul was the great, great, great, great grandson of BillyRay, the one who protected his Masta's family.

"You better pack up and get out of here 'cause she goan get y'all Wellingtons."

"JeanAnn, calm down and tell me what you talkin' 'bout."

The two officers sit down as JeanAnn tells them the story of Granny Haint. When JeanAnn finishes, the two officers get up and start walking towards their car. Douglas asks Jean,

"Why you the only one leaving and none of yo other kin' not followin' you?"

JeanAnn shrugs her shoulders and says, "Ask them."

As they are leaving, Bady tells JeanAnn not to leave until after the investigation is over.

As the officers leave, they pass an old man who is sitting on the porch chewing on some tobacco. He spits in an old coffee can that looks like it has not been washed in years. After wiping the excess spit off his mouth with his sleeve he says, "With RayPaul gone, it's goan get mighty hainey 'round chere." These words send chills down the spine of both officers.

Chapter XVIII

The two officers get into thier car and drive off. As they are driving off the African American version of the Wellingtons estate, they slow down and stop to talk to Curtis Alford, who lives a few houses down from JeanAnn. Bady stops and winds the window down and screams out to Curtis, "What do ya say dair boy?"

They both say this at the same time, as Curtis Alford extends his arm into the car to shake Bady's hand as well. Bady and Curtis Alford used to play on the same football team. They also used to play with each other as young boys. Bady asks Curtis Alfred, "Do you know what's going on 'round here with this killing and spook shit?"

Curtis Alfred's expression quickly changes because of the question Bady has just asked him. It plum wipes the smile clean off his face. Curtis Alfred swallows and says, "I would not be calling her no spook shit, and y'all betta respect Granny cuz' she's back for blood. I ain't got no mo' ta say," as he turns around and begins walking from the dirt road, back to his house. Bady yells out to Alford, "Why you ain't packin' and high tailin' it out here like JeanAnn?" Curtis Alford turns around and yells back, "I believe in Granny and I ain't did nothin' to her," which makes the smile return to his face.

Curtis Alford is a tall, evenly built African American man. He has a small afro which he keeps shaped up with care. He always has a happy go lucky look on his face, which fits him well. He is always wearing overalls to work in because that's all he likes to do. As he answers Bady's question he continues to walk away so he does not have to answer any more. Douglas motions for Bady to pull off. As they pull off from Curtis Alford they get quiet and both have what JeanAnn and the old man told them earlier, running through their minds. They don't quite know what to do with the information.

145

Bady breaks the silence by shouting out, "I don't believe in that nigga spook shit! Douglas jumps from Bady's sudden outburst, which startles him.

"Douglas, now don't you let that nigga spook shit get ta ya. If that is RayPaul that is dead he done did somethin' to somebody and they kill him."

"Bady, you know that's him; that shiny thing we saw in the bodies' head was the quarter JeanAnn said RayPaul keeps in his ear. I'm going to talk to my big brother about what JeanAnn said and ask him what he knows about it." They continue down the old dirt road as night falls in this country town.

The two men drive down the old country road leaving a cloud of dust as the sun drops over the horizon. It is night fall as an old beaten up truck pulls into the trailer park. It is Glenn, RoseMary's husband, coming home drunk after being beaten up by Thadeus, RoseMary's oldest brother. He stops his truck in front of Rosemary's trailer. He stumbles out of his truck and staggers to the front door. He bangs on the door hollering, "Rose, Rose, let me in baby, cuz' I miss you so!" Rose comes to the window rubbing her eyes because she has been awakened.

She responds, "Glenn, go on about your business. I told you not to come back until you got a job." "Baby, baby, come on, open the dowe cuz' I got somethin good furr ya."

"No, no, Glenn this time I'm a sticken to my guns. I told you don't come back unless you got a job." Rose slams the window down and goes back to bed. Glenn really gets mad and starts screaming out, "You spoiled little bitch, who the fuck do you think you are? You ain't got no job. Your brother takes care of you and that spoiled rotten bastard you call a son, fuck all y'alll!"

He stumbles behind a trailer and heads down toward a drainage ditch that crosses the trailer park. He stops down at a stream of water at the bottom of the ditch to relieve himself from the alcohol and beer he consumed earlier. First he hears chains rattling then he hears humming: "Wade in the water, wade in the water, children." He hollers out, "This trailer park don't allow no niggas in it!" Glenn looks around to see where the humming is coming from. "You heard me, nigga, get out!"

As he zips his fly, he feels as though something is standing behind him. The humming has toned down, but it is right in his ear. His stomach begins to growl from the bad smell that surrounds him. He slowly turns around. His eyes pop out of his head from what he is seeing. Granny whispers in his ear, "I don't allow no crackers to tell me where to go."

She has the body of a ram, with horns coming out of her head, spiraling to a point down around her neck, pointing past her face. Her fangs are dripping saliva, and are poking out her mouth. They are very sharp and pointy at the ends. She turns her head and rams Glenn right in the gut with her horns. He hits the ground after being gored and rammed. He tries to scream out but the blood seeping out of his mouth muffles his scream. Granny then continues to slash and ram Glenn's lifeless body. All that could be heard is the ripping of clothes and the tearing of flesh. Then Granny trots off wagging her tail, disappearing into the woods.

The two officers arrive at the sheriff's department to check out for the day. They both get in their own cars and leave in opposite directions. Douglas arrives at his house, opens his door, puts his gun away and flops down on the couch after a long bizarre day. He picks up the phone and begins dialing. "Hello Thadeus. What do you know about that nigga boogie man shit? Daddy did not tell you about your great, great, great, great grand daddy?"

"Yea Douglas, but I don't remember; it was a long time ago. Well, you know our great, great, great, great granddaddy had slaves and he killed all of them. Granny Haint, who he had a whole heap of children with, put a hex on him. They say she was raised by a village's witch doctor. That's how she knew how to hex our great granddaddy. They say one of the slaves stopped Granny from killing our great granddaddy's family. They also say that Granny was really upset because her own kin' stopped her from killing great granddaddy's family. Before she left, she said, 'Fo generations after next, I will get.'"

Douglas sits there thinking and counting his fingers at the same time. He knows about the story but just wants someone else to tell him, so he won't be alone knowing the truth.

"Thadeus, if it's fo generations after next, then she talkin' 'bout us. JeanAnn told me and Bady the same thing you just said."

"Douglas, I don't believe in none of that nigga spook shit. You can let this ruin your evening if you want to."

"Well Thadeus, I am going to call Robert in Chicago and see what he knows."

"Well Douglas, if you believe in that stuff, you better be calling BillyRay to warn him."

147

"Why BillyRay?"

"BillyRay is the name of the slave that saved great granddaddy's family from being killed by the Haint. It just so happens that our nephew has the same name."

"It ain't no just so happens Thadeus, RoseMary named him that on purpose." "Well Thadeus, I believe in it now and I am going to warn BillyRay. I am also still going to call Robert and let him know what's going on."

"Well Douglas, suit yourself. I'll call you later."

Both brothers hang up their phones. Thadeus starts doing work at his desk in his office without a worry in the world. Douglas's head slumps down on the arm of the couch with a dazed look on his face. He knows about the story, he is just in denial of the truth.

The next morning there are two boys playing with homemade boats in one of the drainage streams. One of them notices someone at the bottom of the hill, in the drainage ditch, not far from the water. In fact, part of what they are seeing is in the water and on land. One boy tells the other, "Let's go down there and rob that drunk bum."

Robbing and stealing is a familiar theme in this trailer park. They both stand in shock at what they see. One of the boys falls in a state of shock; the other boy grabs him and pulls him away as they both run to get help. It is the slashed and mangled remains of Glenn.

The sheriff department's phone begins to ring off the hook. The sheriff picks up the phone and says, "What can I do you furr this monin'?"

The sheriff's expression changes as he listens to the caller. After he hangs up the phone he screams, "What in the Sam's hell is goin' on 'round here!"

He then calls Douglas and Bady and orders them to go over to the trailer park and investigate this new murder.

Bady pulls up in his police car he took home over night to pick up Douglas. Douglas leaves his police car at home figuring that it is safer to ride with Bady. When Douglas gets in the car Bady says, "Before you go talkin' 'bout that nigga spook shit let's go over there and investigate." Douglas does not say anything. He just sits there with a bewildered look on his face, which by now is becoming a normal expression.

As they pull up, there are people standing around the body pointing their fingers at it. They all are standing at a distance from it; they wouldn't dare get close to it. As the two officers look at the mangled remains, Douglas notices something.

"I think that's Glenn."

"How do you know, Douglas? cuz' that bodies' really mashed up."

"See that belt buckle? Glenn won it in one of those prison rodeos some time back. Matter of fact, I know that is Glenn cuz', there ain't another one like it."

"Douglas, I hope your brother didn't tear into him. You know they were at it the other day." "My brother mighta stabbed him, but this boy been 'cut inta apple toppins'. My brother ain't did that." We need to get that investigator down here from Jackson to see if they can find some clues that we may have missed."

"He 'spose to be here this monin."

Douglas says, "Bady, look at that green stuff on the body."

Bady takes a stick and pokes it into the green ooze that's on the body. They could smell it before they could pull it to their noses. Bady quickly drops the stick after realizing that this is the foul smell they have been smelling lately and the same smell everyone's been talking about. It is the smell of rotten eggs combined with burnt matches. As other officers arrive one of them tells Bady and Douglas that the investigator is at the headquarters and the sheriff wants them back at the office. Bady and Douglas jump in the car and are on their way to the police department.

When they arrive there is a very well dressed African American man sitting with the sheriff. As Douglas and Bady walk into the room the investigator stands up as if he is anticipating their arrival. The man introduces himself, "My name is Youseph Ali Sunnington. I am the chief forensic investigator from Jackson. I was sent here to help out with this case. Douglas and Bady look at each other with amazement. They are not used to seeing a black man in this high position. They live in a part of the south that has not changed much in its racial attitudes; this region is tucked away, where nobody even really knows the place exists.

Mr. Sunnington says, "You guys all right? It looks like you guys just seen a ghost."

Mr. Sunnington is a tall, well-built African American. He is clean cut and always has a very serious look on his face. His thick, well groomed mustache's movements are controlled by the different expressions his face makes. His movements and his demeanor are like those of a man who is totally in control of his surroundings. Bady and Douglas nod their heads no, they have been affected by the murders that have taken place in this small country town. The sheriff tells the two officers to take Mr. Sunnington to the morgue and explain to him the details about the homicides. The three men walk out the door towards their car.

As they drive, they start conversing on the way. Bady starts, "Well Mr. Sangington,"

"No, my name is not Sangington, it's Sunnington."

"Anyways, we have the remains of one of the victim at the morgue."

"One of the bodies?" replies Mr. Sunnington, "I thought there was only one body."

"Well, we had another murder last night, or this mornin'. Or rather I should say we found another body this mornin'."

"Well, let's head over to the scene that's fresh and undisturbed," advises Mr. Sunnington.

The three men drive over to the trailer park. No one is talking. The only sound in the car is the chatter from the radio. Other than the chatter coming from the radio, there is complete silence. When the three men reach the crime scene they take over and have the officers assisting the investigation stop their duties and they begin assisting in crowd control. Mr. Sunnington takes out his kit and begins taking samples and putting them in small plastic bags. Douglas and Bady stand patiently, making sure no one gets past them and get too close to the crime scene.

After collecting samples from this crime scene Mr. Sunnington wants to go to the first crime scene. The three men walk down the hill and jump over a ditch before climbing a small hill that leads to the road. Mr. Sunnington begins to collect samples there also. He tells Bady and Douglas, "This is not where he was initially killed." He begins following a trail that the other two officers could not see. It leads them from the tall grass where the body was initially found, across a dirt road, and back into the woods that is at the edge of the trailer park. The men come to a complete stop. Douglas looks around and reminisces.

"We used to play around here when we visited grand ma and grand pa.

Come ta think of it, I remember that foul smell when we played here and also hearing chains rattle. We would get these real odd feelings also."

The Wellington family built homes on different parts of the old plantation. They let the original mansion and Granny's home lay in ruins.

"Mama and daddy did not like us over here either."

Mr. Sunnington says, "This is the spot where he was killed. See these hoof prints, old blood and this green substance that I collected from both scenes?"

Bady says to Mr. Sunnington, "Smell it, it has an odd smell to it."

As Mr. Sunnington opens the bag to smell it Bady is trying really hard not to laugh. Mr. Sunnington snatches the bag quickly away from his face with a horrid expression. Bady and Douglas start laughing.

"Come on man, you're not right!," says Mr. Sunnington after smelling the foul substance in the bag.

Mr. Sunnington points and shows the two officers where the body was dragged from. Douglas motions to Mr. Sunnington and Bady to come with him and check on RoseMary and BillyRay.

When they arrive, Rose is crying on her sons shoulder while he verbally consoles her. Douglas eases up to his sister to console her as well. She turns from her son's embrace and welcomes her brother by crying on his chest.

"It's all my fault," says Rose, "I should have never made him stay out. I should've let him in last night".

"Little sis', you mean you saw him last night?"

"Yes, he was drunk; I did not let him in because I wanted him to get a job."

"What time was that?"

"It was after midnight."

BillyRay pulls Bady aside while Rose and Douglas are talking and asks him, "Bady who dat dressed up nigga with y'all?"

"He's one of those big shot investigators from Jackson."

"He looks like just another dressed up nigga to me" replies BillyRay.

Mr. Sunnington steps up to Rose and begins to ask her a few routine questions. He then walks over to BillyRay and asks him, "When was the last time you saw Glenn?"

"I don't allow no niggas to question me," replies Billy.

"Listen here boy; for all I know, you could have got tired of your stepfather abusing your mother; you could have killed him. I could arrest you and lock you up until this investigation is over."

Douglas steps toward Mr. Sunnington and BillyRay to intervene. Before he could get a word out Mr. Sunnington says to him, "Don't say another word, I was sent down here to take over this investigation. Unless your nephew cooperates, I will lock his ass up right now."

BillyRay puts both his arms out so he can get hand cuffed, "Like I said, I don't allow no niggas to question me"

Mr. Sunnington is really fed up with BillyRay. He steps in front of the brash young man and says, "Call me a nigga one mo' ginn, I don't give a dam who you are related to!"

BillyRay looks down at his feet and does not say another word. He knows Mr. Sunnington means business. Mr. Sunnington walks away to blow off a little steam. Douglas tells BillyRay, "Black or not, he is still the law and you better respect him as such." BillyRay leans back on the trailer looking in the direction Mr. Sunnington went and says, "Like I said, ain't no niggas questioning me." He makes the statement this time without the base and mean spirit in his voice.

"Rose, do you remember that story about our great, great, great great grand pa?" asks Douglas. "Yea, I remember that story well. In fact, the slave that saved his family is who I named BillyRay after."

Douglas tells Billy, "Boy, did you know that?"

"Did I know what?" replies BillyRay.

"You always talkin' bout niggas and you are named after one. You see, BillyRay, in dem days the masta use to take up with his slave women. Great, great, great, great grand dad had fourteen or fifteen children by a couple of dem. We some distant kin' to some of dem. If you really want to know the truth, RayPaul was some kin' to you."

BillyRay's face starts getting red. It is obvious he does not like what he is hearing. He yells out, "I don't want to hear that shit! I ain't no kin' ta no niggas!"

He runs up the steps to his trailer and slams the door. Bady looks at Douglas with a big smile and says, "I told you Douglas, y'all some kin' to those black Wellingtons."

"Little sis," says Douglas, "We don't want you to get spooked, but you better be careful 'cause somethin' just ain't right."

Rose answers back, "I feel the same way. I broke out in a cold sweat. It was like something went through my body, after I sent Glenn on his way."

Bady has been standing there with his arms crossed, listening to the conversation between Rose and Douglas before speaking out in a short, loud outburst, "Listen, we got a lot of business to tend to. That investigator gotta get more samples of evidence from the other body down at the morgue. It ain't professional on our part to have him waitin' 'round on us while we talk 'bout that hoodoo shit. Let's go!"

Douglas hugs his sister, and he and Bady begin to walk away. He turns around and motions to Rose that he will call her later by pointing his thumb in his ear and his pointing finger by his mouth. They both walk very fast to their car where Mr. Sunnington is waiting. The three of them jump in the police car and head to the morgue. There is complete silence in the car until it is broken by Douglas asking Mr. Sunnington a question.

"Mr. Sunnington, do you believe in ghosts and evil spirits?"

"Well Douglas, I am supposed to think like a Scientist. If something can't be proven by using the scientific method, then it's not supposed to be real. On the other hand, man does not know everything. I do believe in good spirits and evil spirits. I am a devout Muslim and I believe in Allah or God."

"You one of dem mooslums people?" asks Douglas with a tone of surprise in his voice.

"Why do you ask me that question, Officer Douglas, does it make a difference?"

"I was raised in a Pena costal church and changed faiths when I got older. "God is God!"

"I think those murders were done by an evil spirit," says Douglas.

"What do you mean?"

Douglas begins telling Mr. Sunnington the whole story about Granny Haint. Bady shrugs his shoulders as if he is tired of hearing the story over and over again. When Douglas finishes telling the story to Mr. Sunnington, an odd look appears on his face. Mr. Sunnington replies, "We will have to collect as much information and evidence as possible. After the physical evidence is sent to the lab we will then get feedback from it; we will have a better idea of what we are working with."

The three men walk into the hospital, which is also where the morgue is located, to examine the body. The Hospital is in Springfield Mississippi not far from Brookhaven and not far from Bogue Chitto. Mr. Sunnington asks both officers to wear masks and to put cream under their noses to guard against the stench. Mr. Sunnington begins doing the work of a forensic investigator. Bady and Douglas stand watching Mr. Sunnington nip, probe, smear, and analyze material from the body. The last item he puts in a plastic bag is the quarter out of the ear of RayPaul. After the investigation of the second body, he puts away material to be analyzed at the lab back in Jackson. He then takes off his apron, mask and gloves to wash up. After washing his arms and hands he begins scratching his head in confusion due to what he has just discovered. He begins to anticipate the onslaught of questions that he is going to be asked by Bady and Douglas.

Bady asks, "Well, Sunnington, what have you come up with?"

"Well, believe it or not, looks like this body's been trampled by an animal. There are hoof prints all over this body, in and around both murder scenes. I also found samples of two different types of hair from both bodies, neither one is human. The lab will determine it for sure. I also found this very smelly, greenish substance on both bodies. I have never witnessed anything like this before in my life. I have done many investigations all over this state and two others. I am the very best at what I do. What I've been exposed to here is very new to me. This stuff is starting to give me the Willies." I was a detective before getting trained in forensics and again this is all new to me.

"I told you Bady, there is something here the likes that we ain't never seen before," says Douglas.

"Douglas, this stuff is starting to get to me also." I think I need some of that moonshine."

The three men leave the morgue going back to the sheriff's department. They all arrive at the sheriff's office and fill him in on what they have discovered thus far. Mr. Sunnington tells the men that he has to leave in order to get this evidence to the lab in Jackson. He walks out the door and takes off. Sheriff Bodine, officers Bady and Douglas sit in the office with blank looks on their faces. They do not know what to make of the information they were just given. The two deputies walk out of the sheriff's office not saying anything. They both get into their cars like zombies and pull out of the parking lot, going in opposite directions.

Chapter XIX

At the trailer park, people are walking around very cautiously. No one is walking alone. BillyRay is engaged in a conversation with his mother Rose. He is getting ready to leave the trailer park. The conversation is going on while he is walking out the door.

"BillyRay, where do ya think you goin' with all these murders goin' on 'round here?"

"Ma, um just walkin' to the stowe and back."

"To the stowe!" "What the hell you need from the stowe? It will be dark by the time ya get back. That's when all this shit is happenin'."

"I know, I know ma', ain't nothing going to happen to me. If anything comes my way, um goin' ta kick 'em, punch him and grab the nearest thang and bust it ova' its head."

As BillyRay is saying this, he is throwing punches and kicks in the air demonstrating what he is going to do.

"Ma, I ain't scared of no niggas, especially no dead ones."

Rose watches as her son disappears around the corner of the next trailer. The streets seem to get emptier with every step he takes. The inhabitants of the trailer park seem to be frightened by the murders that have been taking place in and around the trailer park. They all seem to have the same panic stricken faces as they lock into the beat of darkness. Douglas arrives home and gets out of his car and walks in his house. As he is walking, he is cautiously watching his surroundings. He nervously puts his key in the lock to open the door. He quickly turns on the lights and shuts the door at the same time. He grabs his recliner and puts it in the corner of the living room so nothing can come up from behind. He pulls the coffee table with the phone on it closer, so he would not have to stretch the cord. He picks up the phone and begins dialing his brother Thadeus's number.

"Hello, Thadeus, did you know they found Glenn dead in the trailer park?"

"No, I did not know that."

"I have to ask you anyways, did ya have anything to do with Glenn's murder?"

"Now Douglas, ya know I would'nt do a thang like that. I can't stand him; I'd beat the hell out of um; but I would neva' killum'.

"I know, I know, Thadeus; you would never do a thang like that. Well, anyways, you won't believe what the investigator found out so far about the murders."

Thadeus reacts, "Get on with it, get on with it. I won't say anything about your private police information."

"Well Thadeus, the investigator found hairs that were not human all over both bodies and there were hoof prints on RayPaul's body.

"How do you know that's RayPaul?"

"First of all, there was a quarter in the ear of the first victim. RayPaul is the only one that does that. His wife told us he ain't been home in a couple of days, which ain't like him. Anyways, the investigator also found this green smelly fluid all over both bodies. He told us he will know what the fluid is after it's examined at the lab. He also took dental prints, the best that he could, to identify the victims. He said Glenn was like humpty, dumpty; it would take a whole lot of people to put him back together again. Thadeus I am getting scared."

"Douglas, how can you get scared with that cannon in your hostler. Give me a break." "Thad, I wanna stay over your house tonight."

"Well Douglas, if it makes you feel any better, come on over. I'm getting in the hot tub; the front dowe will be open."

Douglas leaves his house in the same cautious way as he came. He usually leaves his firearm at home, but tonight he has it strapped on.

BillyRay is walking like he always does without a care in the world. The road that leads to the store is parallel to the high way, which has a thin strip of woods that is about thirty yards wide between them. As he walks he hears the zooming of cars from the nearby highway. In between the noise of the cars he hears the chirping of crickets and sees flashes from fire flies. He turns right on another dirt road that leads to an old country store. As he gets closer to the store he sees someone standing in the door yelling something and waving their hands inwards. As he gets even closer, he sees that it is the store owner saying, "Hurry up, hurry up BillyRay, um a closin' soon." The store's owner is looking around very nervously while BillyRay gets what he wants to buy.

"Mr. Tom, you usually stay open an hour later than this."

"Well BillyRay, all this murdering going on, ain't nobody comin' out this late much. I work here alone this time of night and um gettin' out of here befo' dark."

"I don't believe in none of that nigga spook shit and I ain't definantly in no hurry," states BillyRay "Well, I am. Now, get what you gonna get, cuz' I got to go. From what I hear tell, yo family got something to do with that stuff. You should be scared."

BillyRay pays for his candy, potato chips and ice cream while the store owner packs his bag. The store owner drops the money in the register as he hands BillyRay his bag. He walks BillyRay to the door. As soon as BillyRay is out the door, it slams, and seconds after, clicks of locks being set can be heard. BillyRay looks back at the door as if Mr. Tom was crazy. BillyRay starts walking down the road. He is getting a little nervous himself, so he cuts through the tall grass that leads to the road that will take him home. He has to walk about one hundred fifty yards to get there. As he walks he notices something. He hears no chirping from crickets and sees no flashes from fire flies. This disturbs him and he begins to walk faster. He inhales through his nostrils and the expression on his face gets distorted from the intense foul smell. He has smelled this foul scent before. He also hears the rattling of chains knowing there are no animals in sight. His mind races as he tries to remember where he smelled this scent before. His heart starts racing because it hits him, that this is the same odor he smelled when he and RayPaul were talking. He begins to hear humming. This is the same hymn that he and RayPaul heard the night RayPaul was killed.

BillyRay yells out, "I don't know who you are, but you people ain't got no business 'round these parts!" There is the sound of crackling grass, as it begins to part behind him. The humming begins to get closer and BillyRay starts to run as fast as he can. He sees a set of headlights through the grass, and continues running, as fast as, he possibly can, toward them. The humming and the noise from the parting grass gets closer and closer.

BillyRay is almost out of the woods. When he steps onto the dirt road he trips and falls after stepping in a deep pot hole. He lands on his back. Contents of the bag fly everywhere. The moment he hits the ground, she's already standing over him. The bright lights from an oncoming car enables BillyRay to look into her eyes. She has the body of a goat, or sheep, a distorted human face that has smelly green ooze coming out a hole in the center of her head, and saliva dripping in BillyRays' face from her long pointed teeth. She says, "Fo' generations after next, I will get!" then backs up and disappears.

The car comes to a screeching halt and someone quickly jumps out to help BillyRay to his feet. It is Douglas, BillyRay's uncle that has come to his rescue. BillyRay jumps to his feet with the help of his uncle. He gets into the police car and quickly slams down the lock on the door. Douglas gets in on the other side and slams his door.

"Did you see it, did you see it?"

"See what?"

"The boogey lady!"

"I saw something, but it took off as I got closer."

"Yea uncle, it had the body of a goat or sheep, with white eyes and horns coming out her head. She was also slobbering on me with her sharp teeth and bad breath. She told me Fo' generation after next, I will get'."

"Come on BillyRay, you been watching too many of those horror flicks."

BillyRay turns to his uncle with tears and fear in his eyes, and beads of sweat running down his face and says, "Uncle, I know what I saw, please believe me."

In Douglas's mind, he believes everything his nephew has said. What came out of Douglas's mouth were words to ease his nephew into the same denial that Douglas externally displays. While Douglas and BillyRay spin dust from their tires as they are leaving the scene of almost another death, Granny Haint has other plans. She jumps through the tall grass that leads to the woods that borders the trailer park. She begins to talk out loud, *He thinks he got away. Um o get that little big mouth disrespectful scoundrel. Um o get his mama first. She named him after the bastard that stop my pain the first time. He always bad mouthin' me and my peoples. He and she dam show got to go!*

As she trots to the trailer, Granny looks around to make sure no one is looking. She has the body of a ram with horns in a spiral formation going from the top of her head spiraling around her neck, pointing sharply past her mouth. The little screen door is cracked open so she wedges her horn in and opens it. She then turns the door knob with one of her horns, then she slowly pushes it open. She begins humming "Wade in the Water," as she eases on in the trailer. RoseMary's room is at the end of the hallway, to the left. On the opposite side of her room is BillyRay's room.

RoseMary is awakened by humming. She rubs her eyes and as she rises from her slumber she yells out, "BillyRay, I done told you stop mocking that old woman. She gonna get you!" Her bedroom's door is shut and locked in fear of the unknown. As she sits up, she hears chains rattling and she smells that terrible smell, which changes her facial features. Granny begins to trot building up speed, knocking down whatever is in her way. She comes around the corner and speeds through the door. Rose is sitting up in her bed when Granny, with all force, rams Rose's door into her. RoseMary lands on the floor against her bedroom wall, and then Granny smashes her again. Granny rams her so hard that the print of her body can be seen outside the trailer.

Rose's whole chest and the bottom of her chin has been smashed in beyond recognition. Granny looks down at her and says "You were right, um goan get him too. I just had to get the bitch that birthed him first." Granny spits and leaves trotting slowly wagging her little tail, as if she has done nothing wrong. The screen door that is in front of the main entrance of the trailer is latched, so Granny rams it off one of its hinges, and walks out the door. She trots toward the back of the trailer and disappears in the woods of the old Wellington plantation.

Douglas and BillyRay are almost at Thadeus's house. Just before they turn the corner, Douglas eyes open wide. He yells out, "Oh my God, Rose!" The expression on BillyRay's face goes from fear to frustration of uncertainty. BillyRay yells out, "Douglas, hurry and turn around. We got to get back to my mama!" Douglas turns the car around like a dare devil race car driver. He is not worried about doing this illegal maneuver because he is the law.

They pull into the entrance of the trailer park as if they were on the last lap of a stock car race. When they reach the trailer BillyRay jumps out the car before it could be put in park. Douglas jumps out the car yelling at BillyRay to hold up until he gets there. BillyRay hesitantly waits as Douglas catches up with him. When they reach the trailer they notice that the screen door is hanging on one hinge and the front door is half way open. BillyRay knows his mother never leaves the front door open. Douglas pulls his gun out with one hand and grabs BillyRay by the shoulder and pulls him behind him. BillyRay is not pleased with this because he wants to see if his mother is alright. Douglas cautiously walks up the few steps that lead into the trailer. His gun sways from left to right, in anticipation of anything that may come his way.

Douglas pushes the door open the rest of the way with his foot. BillyRay follows; mocking his uncle's every move. As Douglas goes into the interior of the trailer he immediately notices little bloody hoof prints coming out of Rose's room leading out the trailer. Douglas puts his forearm on BillyRay's chest to halt him. Douglas continues to walk down the hall leading to Rose's room. When he reaches her bedroom, he is in fear of what he does not want to see. He jumps into the room pointing his gun to the left and right. He is looking in horror as he sees his sister's lifeless body. He backs out of the room covering his eyes. BillyRay tries to push past his uncle to see for himself. Douglas does not want him to see the carnage, so he tries to hold BillyRay back.

BillyRay yells out, "Get the fuck off me uncle, let me go, now!" BillyRay's determination allows him to push past his uncle and he goes into his mother's room. He screams out, "Noooooo!" Inside the room Rose's lifeless body is smashed into the wall of the trailer. Her face, chest and shoulder look like she has been struck several times by a sledge hammer. Douglas and BillyRay walk back outside after witnessing the dreadful sight of their sister and mother in this condition. They both stumble out of the trailer with their heads down, following the little bloody hoof prints.

The prints lead into the interior of the trailer park, then into the woods. Douglas looks up at BillyRay and says, "These prints are heading toward the old Wellington mansion. This is as far as I'm going without back up." BillyRay looks at his uncle in agreement. The two distraught individuals turn around constantly looking behind themselves as they walk back to the police car. They are hurt, and their hearts are heavy. BillyRay looks over to his uncle and asks, "What will we do next?" "I think we need to learn more about Granny and I know just where to go," answers Douglas. Douglas picks up the mouth piece to his radio and radios the headquarters to alert the officers that are on duty of what just happened, so the trailer can be secured before someone tries to wonder in.

Chapter XX

Douglas and BillyRay are heading over to RayPaul's house to question JeanAnn again about Granny Haint. Uncle it's late, do you think they're up? If they ain't, they will be

"Well BillyRay, we are going over to JeanAnn's house to get more information about Granny. She was ret ta high tail it out of here until Bady and I told her to stay put until after the investigation." BillyRay did not have much to say. He just sat there with tears running down his face. They arrive at RayPaul's house and find JeanAnn and her uncle sitting on the porch trying to catch a breeze on this hot Mississippi night. Douglas and BillyRay get out their car and step up on the porch.

"Well JeanAnn, we just found my sister in her house dead."

JeanAnn shakes her head saying, "Lord have mercy."

"Do you know anything more about Granny Haint that you ain't tellin' us 'bout?"

When Douglas starts telling JeanAnn about Rose, she stands up anticipating what Douglas is going to say. She plops back in her chair as she tells Douglas, "Yes, yes, I do know more about Granny Haint. RayPaul had been seeing her two weeks before his death. When he told me that he was seeing her, I did not believe him until I saw her myself"

"You saw her!" shouts Douglas.

"Yes, I most certainly did. I stayed up late one night waitin' for RayPaul to come home. It was a Friday night and RayPaul neva comes straight home on pay day. I was sitin' in my chair when I heard scuffling on my back porch. It sounded like two people. I thought it was RayPaul comin' home drunk with one of his drunk buddies to spend the night. You know that's how RayPaul was, he kind hearted like that. I grabbed one of the kid's bats and tip toed to the back dowe. I snatched the dowe open and there she was a mule with the head of a human. She had pasty white eyes, green stuff coming out a hole in her forehead. She also had a very bad odor. It smelled like rotten eggs. She said, 'I don't want you, I want RayPaul. Ya see, RayPaul is the only one that can stop me, so I got to stop him first.' Well Douglas, RayPaul told me he was going to warn y'all the same night he disappeared. He told me the Haint gonna get all you Wellingtons."

Douglas replies, "How we gonna stop her? What do we do?"

"I don't right know," replies JeanAnn. "I think y'all need to see the Root Lady, yonder in those woods."

JeanAnn points in the direction where the Root Lady lives. "I would not go over there tonight cuz' she don't like to be disturbed at night. Go there first thang in the monin'."

Douglas thanks JeanAnn for giving him the information about Granny. He and Billy start walking back to the car. As they change directions to open their car doors, they are facing the porch. They both stop to listen to what JeanAnn's uncle was about to say. "I done told y'all it was goan get mighty Hainy 'round chere." He begins to laugh with his deep voice, which gives Douglas and BillyRay the creeps.

The two look at each other in dismay. They get in the car and back out the driveway not knowing where they are going or what they are going to do. There is silence in the car as they leave JeanAnn's house. They both seem affected by the comment that the old man on the porch has made. Their faces have the look of grief and fear on them. The silence is broken by the ringing of the phone. They both are spooked by the breakage of silence. Douglas picks up the phone.

"Who would you like to speak to?" Douglas pauses as he listens to the person on the other end.

"Well Thadeus, I guess you haven't heard, the Haint done killed RoseMary. Hello, hello!"

Thadeus just hangs up the phone after hearing the news.

"Uncle Douglas, I think Uncle Thadeus is heading over to my house. Let's meet him there. Uncle, I think you need to turn on your radio 'cause someone maybe trying to contact us."

Douglas reaches down and turns on the radio in the squad car. As soon as it comes on Douglas and BillyRay hear, "Douglas, Douglas do you read me?"

Douglas picks up the mouth piece and speaks back. "I copy,"

"Douglas, where in the hell have you been? I called your house and your cell phone and you did not answer. I am here at yo sista Rose's house, gettin' it secured. I don't know what the hell's going on, but I am startin' to believe in that nigga spook shit now. I ain't neva' seen nothin' like this befo' in all my days. The little bloody hoof prints coming out the house is like something out of a horror flick. Are you coming this way?"

"Yea Bady, I am in route as we speak. Thadeus is on his way also.

"I followed the hoof prints out of the trailer and into the woods. They lead to this big old oak tree and then they disappear."

"You mean, that oak tree over, by where the old mansion is?" inquires Douglas.

"Yea, why?"

"Man, you nuts. That's where all this stuff started. Ain't no way in hell I'da went in there without back up. Um surprised she did not get you."

"I had my gun in my hand while I was walkin'. If she would have came out my gun woulda did the talkin'.'"

"Listen Bady, don't do nothin' or go nowhere by yourself. I will be there directly."

As Douglas and BillyRay continue driving towards the trailer park BillyRay asks his uncle a question.

"Does Uncle Bobby know what's going on?"

"I was going to call him and tell him, but all this stuff keeps happenin'. I will call him and tell him after we pay a visit to the Root Lady in the monin'."

163

Chapter XXI

In Chicago Illinois, at a major insurance company, two men work together every day and don't realize what they both have in common. Robert Lewis Wellington is supervised by Marvin Warren Wellington who is the regional district manager. Marvin and Robert often have lunch together and socialize with each other personally. Their sons have played on the same baseball, football and basketball teams since they were old enough to play organized sports. They would often joke about being related but never asking one another where they came from.

On this particular morning they greet each other at the water cooler.

"Good morning Robert."

"Good morning to you to Marvin. How's the family doing?"

"Just fine; and yours?"

"Mine is doing just fine. In fact, Marvin Jr. got straight A's on his report card."

"That's great Marvin, I am going to have to tighten up on Bobby Jr., because he is doing just enough to get by. I keep threatening him with removing him from sports, but it just doesn't seem to be sinkin' in."

"Robert, you will just have to stay on him, he will come around."

"Oh yea, Robert, I am going to need that report by Friday or I am going to catch a bad one from my higher ups. I can help you if you need help."

"Marvin, I will be able to handle it with no problem. I could not ask for a better boss than you." "I am not your boss, God is, we are just coworkers. How's your wife and two daughters?"

"They are doing just fine, and yours?"

"They are doing fine as well my man."

Marvin and Robert Wellington both have a junior, two daughters another son and wives. They have more in common than what they imagine. Marvin is well known in his community. He runs programs for inner city youth that keeps them off the streets. He is also a spoke person for African Americans that have been served injustice.

In Mississippi, Thadeus arrives at Rosemary's trailer. Rose's trailer has had many visitors. Some are wondering what happened, and others are mourning her death, Thadeus, Douglas, BillyRay and Bady meet there at the same time. Thadeus grabs BillyRay and pulls him to his chest with tears in his eyes. He looks BillyRay in the eyes and says,

"Boy, are you all right?" BillyRay does not reply, while holding his uncle tight.

"Douglas, we gonna get the sons of a bitches that killed our sister," says Thadeus while shaking his head in dismay. Bady says, "Has anyone heard from the big shot investigator?"

"He supposed to be here later on this evenin'," replies Douglas, "Me and BillyRay suppose to be going over to that Root Lady's house to see if she can tell us how to stop Granny Haint."

"Y'all act like she is really someone. Stop talkin' that nigga spook shit."

BillyRay, still in his uncles' embrace, sadly looks up at his uncle and says, "Uncle, she is real. I saw her last night."

"Seeing that you said that BillyRay, I think we all need to go over there. At this point, I will do anything to get whoever or whatever is doing the killin'," replies Thadeus.

The four men jump into their cars and start driving towards the Root Lady's house.

Earlier that same morning, the sun light was just rising over the horizon when the Root Lady received a few knocks on the front door of her shack. The knocks were followed by humming and the rattling of chains. Her shack is made of wood with a tin roof. It is small on the outside but very large on the inside. It's like an optical illusion. It is basically one very large room that has a small partition where the Root Lady sleeps. She does not have any electricity and heats her home with a pot belly stove that sits in the middle of her dwelling. All around the stove there is clutter. It looks as though she has been collecting stuff and leaving it in her shack her whole life. Her walls have feathers, bones and other trinkets hanging from them.

She has an altar with melted candles and incense sitting in holders. Above the altar she has shelves lined with mason jars, full of funny looking concoctions.

"Betty Mae, is that you knockin' dis time of monin'?"

The knocks on the door become louder and harder. "Betty Mae, what did I tell you?"

A voice answers back. "If you don't open up this dowe, um gonna kick it down."

The Root Lady's face frowns from the foul smell coming from the other side of the door as she shuffles towards the door to open it. She suddenly stops and says, "That don't sound like no Betty Mae, and I ain't openin' no dowe," as she turns around, heading toward her bedroom.

There is a loud thud and then, a crash. Then there is a clipty clump sound just past the door and into the Root Lady's shack. The Root Lady grabs a machete holding it up in the air next to her head in order to protect herself. She could not believe what was standing before her, it is Granny Haint. Granny spoke out in a loud raspy voice.

"My dealings ain't with you. I don't want you tellin' those white men nothin' 'bout me. I know you work Mojo and you know 'bout me."

As Granny is talking she is looking around the room. Her features are ruff and menacing looking but they seem to soften as she looks around the room. The shack reminds her of her younger days back in the old country.

"If you'n do tell them 'bout me, my dealin's will be with you. You will get what the udens got."

"I ain't goan tell dem nothin'." "They were suppose to come last night but they were told not to. That's what the owl told me."

"I know, cuz' I was dat owl that told ya. My business done wit' ya. Leave them white men be. Yea and 'notha thang, you need to get rid of some of this stuff fo something rubs together and work a Mojo on you." The mule bodied Haint backed up very quickly and disappears. It was like she reversed time because the door she kicked down to get in fixed itself as if nothing had ever happened.

Just as Granny cleared out the four men pull up in three different cars. They park in front of the path that leads up to the Root Lady's shack. She lives in a very wooded area. One would have to take a couple of side roads in order to get to her shack. She likes her seclusion from the outside world. If someone is not designated to go to her house she would never be visited. Thadeus leads the way as the four men walk up the narrow path leading to her shack. On both sides of the path leading to her house there are thickets with prickers and thick impenetrable bushes.

Thadeus knocks on the door with three hard knocks. When Thadeus hits the door on the third knock the three men are standing behind him in a single file. Bady notices something and he taps Douglas on the shoulder and points toward the ground. Douglas' eyes pop wide open with amazement. There are hoof prints all over the ground, the same ones found at the last two crime scenes. Thadeus yells, "Open up, I know you're in there!" A voice yells back, "Y'all go on. I ain't got no dealins' wit y'all!"

Douglas yells, "Listen, we just want to talk ta ya!"

"I said, go the hell on, I ain't talkin' to y'all!"

The men get out of single file and all have irritated looks on their faces. Bady yells, "This is official police business, open up the dowe or we'll kick it in!"

The old squeaky voice responds, "Hold on, hold on, um a comin'."

The men hear clickty, clack and bangs as the old woman shuffles through her cluttered shack to open the door. The door slowly opens and a short purple haired old black woman appears. "What the hell do y'all want?"

She has a long robe with feathered beads around her neck. Her finger nails are longer than her fingers as they curl inwards. She has a pasty brown colored face with few wrinkles. Her teeth are very white and maintained for a woman her age.

"What the hell y'all want?" she asks.

Bady answers back, "Do you know anything about Haints?"

The old women looks at them as if they are bothering her and says, "I don't know nothin' 'bout nothin'."

"We were told that you the Root Lady, and you know all about this kinda stuff."

"I done told y'all, I don't know nothin'. Now leave me be."

She never takes her hand off the door knob while she and Bady are talking. She begins to slowly close the door with every word. Thadeus puts his hand on the door before she can fully close it and says, "We know you know something." The Root Lady replies, "I know two thangs, one you betta get yow hands off my dowe, and two, y'all betta get way from 'round dease parts 'cause y'all don't know what y'all messin wit'."

Thadeus takes his hand off the door. The Root Lady begins to laugh with a hard deep voice, "Ha ha, ha, ha; hee, hee, hee, hee."

The four men turn around in single file and head down the narrow path toward their cars. Bady says, "That old black bitch knows somethin." Douglas looks at Bady and says, "Did you see those hoof prints around the front dowe? Come to think of it, they were the same ones left at all the crime scenes. What is really odd is the hoof prints are not on the path the four men just walked down and they seem to appear only at the front door and nowhere else. "Maybe she paid a visit to the Root Lady to shut her up."

Thadeus has a very irritated look on his face from listening to their conversation about the Haint. He yells out, as if she can hear him, "I don't know if you're real, but if you killed my sista', um goan kill you. You old black nigga bitch!"

He looks over at Douglas and says, "Out of all of us here, I didn't think you, "Mr. Scientific Method college boy would believe in that nigga hoodoo shit!"

Douglas puts his head down and digs his foot back and forth making a mark in the dirt road. "I ain't said I believe in anything. I know things are not right based on the facts we have received and by the way things are happenin'."

"Take this fact down, I'm going to get my gun and hunt whatever or whoever killed my sista; they will be dead befo the rooster crows in the monin'!" replies Thadeus.

Douglas cries out as he watches his brother get into his car, "Now Thadeus, you can't go 'round shootin people. That's what the law is here for!"

Thadeus sticks his head out the window and shouts, "Fuck the law!" Then he pulls off, spinning his tires, leaving a cloud of dust.

Bady gets into his car and Douglas and BillyRay get in theirs. Douglas yells out for Bady to follow him back to the office. They head out on the old country road heading for uncertainty and despair. As they drive by Annie Mae's café they all look at the African American juke joint in shock and amazement because there is always something stirring there but today it is as quiet as a church house on a Monday. Douglas pulls his cell phone out of his pocket and hands it to BillyRay. He tells BillyRay to look up his Uncle Robert's phone number, dial it and hand it back to him. BillyRay finds his uncle's number dials it and hands it to him. Douglas waits as the phone rings and the person on the other side picks up.

"Robert, Robert, how are you doing?"

"I'm ok Douglas; you sound stressed."

"I am stressed. I have some bad news, Rose is dead."

Robert yells out, "What!"

His coworkers stand up in their cubicles to see who caused the sudden outburst. Robert immediately leaves his cubical and heads towards the men's room where he can stress his concerns more freely. He yells back at Douglas,

"How did it happen!"

"Robert, what I'm about to tell you, it's going to be hard for you to believe."

As Douglas begins to explain everything to his brother in detail, BillyRay slumps down in his seat and begins to cry again. When Douglas finishes Robert can't believe what he just heard.

"Douglas, I remember that tale about Granny Haint. I can't, and I don't believe it. I am going to get my family together and get down there as soon as I can."

"Robert, I would leave your family home, if I were you."

"Douglas, I don't believe in none of that shit. I 'm going to bring my family down to pay respect to their auntie. We will be down there as soon as possible."

Robert hangs up the phone as tears run down his cheeks. He walks back to his cubical with a limp and sluggish demeanor. He plops down in his chair with a blank look on his face, staring at the wall of his cubical. Marvin, Roberts's boss walks by and notices the look on Robert's face. He stops to see what is wrong with his fellow coworker.

"Robert, what's the matter?"

"It's a long story Marv'."

"Robert, come to my office after lunch so that we can talk."

"I will be there directly after lunch."

The two men acknowledge each other with the nod of their heads. Little do they know that they have more in common with each other than just their job. They will discover this at the meeting they will have after lunch.

Chapter XXII

Marvin is sitting behind his desk looking at reports when he hears three knocks. He answers, "Come in." It is Robert still feeling down in the dumps about the loss of his sister. Marvin tells Robert to have a seat. Robert sits down and looks Marvin in the face before he begins to speak.

"Marvin, I have to go to Mississippi to attend my sister's funeral."

"What part of Mississippi? I'm asking because I have to leave soon too. My uncle died a few days ago."

"I'm going to BrookHaven, what about you?"

"I'm going not far from there; I'm going to Bogue Chitto."

"My uncle got brutally murdered almost a week ago."

"So was my sister."

There is silence as they both contemplate whether they should tell each other what they know. They look at one another and both say at the same time,

"There is something strange about those murders."

Marvin asks, "What do you mean?"

Robert says, "You tell me first."

"Well, there is this story about my great, great, great, great grandmother, whose family was killed by her masta. She turned into this creature we call a Haint, and she tried to kill masta's family. One of her grandchildren hid and was protective of his masta's family stopped her. Because he stopped her she vowed to get revenge."

"Do you believe in that stuff, Marvin?"

"Oh yea, I definitely believe in it. It ain't nothing to play with. I just have faith in the All Mighty and I live each day by that faith. I think it's strange that we both have to go to funerals at the same time."

"Marvin, I have something even stranger to tell you. The master that killed your great great great great granny was my great great great great grandfather. They called him Grand Daddy Wellington. They say most the children he killed were his own children by your great, great, grand ma'."

"Yea Robert, that's what was told to me also."

"You wanna hear something else Robert?"

"Yea, go ahead."

"I kinda felt a strange closeness to you over the years."

"Why didn't you tell me that before, Marv? I guess this makes us distant cousins or something like that."

"I did not think that it would be that important, and I guess I forgot all together."

"The same here man."

The men hug each other in jest, not knowing how important they would be to one other.

In Mississippi Bady, Douglas and BillyRay head back to the police station where they will meet, evaluate and discuss their next plan of action. BillyRay looks over at his uncle and says, "Uncle Douglas, what did Uncle Robert say about what's going on down here?

"Of course, he is not happy about what happened to our sister and he does not believe in Granny Haint. He said he was going to ask for time off to come to the funeral and all. He wants to bring his whole family but I told him not to."

"Why not bring them? cuz' I ain't seen my little cousins in years."

"They don't need to be exposed to anything with all this killin' goin on down here."

BillyRay presses his forehead on the dash board and begins to cry again. He starts banging his fists on the dashboard, yelling out, "Why, why, why!" Douglas's eyes well up with tears as they drive back towards the police station. When they arrive the sheriff is standing in the doorway as if he knew they were coming. Bady pulls up a moment after. They all open their doors at the same time and get out of their cars. Sherriff greets Douglas with a hug to console him about his loss. The three men follow the sheriff into his office where they are seated by him. The sheriff waddles around the three men to seat himself behind his desk.

The first words out of the sheriff's mouth are, "We have to kill the son of a bitch that is doin the killin' 'round here."

Douglas replies, "What if we can't kill her?"

"Anything and everything can be killed. I don't wanna hear none of that nigga spook shit no mo'. The investigator called and he will be here directly. I suggest we stay put until he gets here. We need to find out what we are working with. He may have some information we can use to catch the killa." BillyRay looks up and says, "What if it's a woman?"

Bady, Douglas, and BillyRay look at each other and all three look at the sheriff hoping to get an answer. The sheriff looks back at the three gentlemen and shakes his head. Baddy gets up because he feels fidgety and walks out the office. He takes a few steps to the right and stands in the middle of the hall with his hands on his hips just staring down the hall that holds a few offices at the end. He smells a nasty odor and frowns as a result. He feels something pressing on his legs then he looks down. It is a big black cat that is rubbing against his legs with its back arched. It does a figure eight between his legs weaving in and out. The cat wraps its tail around his leg like a snake taking hold of its victim. The cat unraps its tail and begins it's sexy and dainty walk down the hall, twirling its tail. Bady stood there in shock and in awe of what just took place. The cat turned and looked back at Bady with its pasty white eyes and big fangs with drool coming off them and fluid coming out its fore head and winks at Bady before disappearing in one of the offices. Bady's hair stands up on the back of his neck. He slowly turns around and has a seat back in the office not saying a word. Sherriff looks at Bady and says "Boy you look like you done seen a ghost." Bady sits there still without any facial expression. Sherriff speaks out again 'Dam boy ya sittin there all dumb founded, what the cat got your tongue?" The sheriff chuckles as they continue to talk. Bady just sits there in shock.

Meanwhile, Thadeus has just arrived back at his house. He gets out of his car and goes through the back door of his medium sized mansion. He heads straight for his bedroom. When he arrives he walks towards the nightstand that is on the right side of his bed. He opens the top drawer and pulls out a .38 revolver and some bullets and begins loading his gun. He quickly turns his head towards the door and begins sniffing the air. He notices a foul smell in the air and hears the rattling of chains and the humming of wade in the water. He then hears scratching at the back door. As well as a mansion he has a small farm on his property. He has horses, pigs, goats, chickens, and prize game cocks that he fights for money.

"I hope dem dam thangs ain't got a loose. They will tear each other ta shreds." He grabs the door knob and snatches it open with a sudden jerk. The door opens and Thadeus' face is full of claws and flapping wings. Thadeus grabs whatever is tearing at his face by its legs and throws it to the ground, in the same motion he runs back toward his room to get his gun. His' face has been badly clawed. The fluff of feathers roll around until it uprights itself. He turns around to look at what did the damage to his face. Granny's head is on the body of a game cock. Her claws are full of flesh and blood as she anxiously prepares herself for Thadeus's death. She has green substance oozing out the middle of her forehead. One of Thadeus' eyes is hanging out of its socket, with blood oozing out of it. He pushes the eye back into place with one hand as he runs back to his room to get his gun. Granny yells out to Thadeus, "You got to do better than that cuz' um oh kill you!"

Thadeus slams the door to his bedroom and locks it; he then grabs his gun off the bed. There is scratching and clawing at the door. Granny is trying to get in Thadeus's room. The scratching stops and there is a sound of scuffling and rolling around on the floor outside the door. Thadeus has his finger on the trigger with one hand and the other hand is holding his eye in place. With his face terribly mauled he yells out, "Come on, you old nigga bitch, um goan blow yo head off!"

There is silence as Thadeus anticipates Granny's onslaught. He hears Granny outside his door. He is thinking that one good shot will split that rooster in two. He hears steps going away from the door. Then he hears something coming towards him very fast. He yells out, "Leave me be or I will blow yo fuckin' head off!"

When the noise is close to his door he begins firing rounds at what he thinks is coming. There is a crash and the door is busted wide open. He turns and tries to reload his gun. Granny hits him, smashing him and the night stand into the wall. She backs up a few times and rams him over and over again. Granny has changed form from a rooster to a ram. As she backs away her horns are full of blood and meshed flesh. She then turns into a mule and kicks him in the face. Before leaving she menacingly stares at Thadeus. As she backs away she spits on Thadeus's lifeless body.

The phone rings at the sheriff's department and someone answers it. The dispatcher comes to the doorway of the sheriff's office and says, "We just received a call and they said they heard shots coming from Thadeus's house." All four men jump up and take off for their cars. Douglas and BillyRay ride in one car and Bady and the sheriff in another.

Turning into the entrance of the estate there are long white fences on both sides of the road leading to Thadeus' house. He has Thorough bred horses that are grazing and frolicking around in the beautiful green grass as they would on any other day. The two cars slowly pull up to the big white house that has six very large pillars holding it up. In fact Thadeus's house is a slightly smaller version of the original Wellington mansion. The three officers get out their cars with their pistols drawn. The sheriff motions with his hand for Douglas to go around the right side. Bady will stay in front and the sheriff will go around the left side of the mansion. BillyRay begins to follow his uncle when Douglas turns around and says,

"BillyRay you ain't got no gun, you need to stay here."

"Why I got to stay here? What if she comes this way? What am I going to do?"

Douglas scratches his head and says, "You got a point there. Just stay behind me."

The four men begin walking slowly to their designated places of entry. They are stalking whatever they think they will find in or around the mansion. Bady crouches behind his police car with his gun pointing at the front door of the mansion. BillyRay crouches behind his uncle mimicking every move he makes, like a shadow. The sheriff with his short Rolly Polly stature still knows how to cover himself, as he stalks his way around the house, gun swaying back and forth with a cigar hanging out the corner of his mouth.

BillyRay and Douglas reach the back door first. Douglas points down at feathers, blood, and two sets of hoof prints in front of the back door entrance, leaving the house. When Douglas steps through the back door he points his gun left, then right, because there are two hallways that are connected by the back door. Douglas and BillyRay see more feathers and blood as they follow the trail of both towards Thadeus's bedroom. The sheriff steps through the back door and Douglas quickly points his gun to where he heard noise coming from. When he realizes that it is the sheriff, he points the gun toward his original destination, Thadeus's room. He quickly steps in the room with his gun pointed. He steps out almost as fast as he stepped in after viewing the carnage. The sheriff walks into the bedroom and then into the adjoining bathroom to make sure everything is safe. When the sheriff realizes everything is ok he puts his gun back into his holster and walks toward the lifeless body.

Thadeus' body is in a sitting position. He is leaning up against the nightstand that absorbed his impact. The back of the night stand has been pushed through the wall. Half of it is outside of the indentation of the impact. Thadeus' head is slumped over the hole which is in his caved in chest. His face is badly mutilated and his eyeball is hanging out, still dripping blood. The sheriff comes back into the room and hugs BillyRay and Douglas. BillyRay tries to pull away to go see his uncle for himself. Douglas grabs BillyRay and says,

"You don't want to see him like that. Please don't go inside there."

The sheriff radios for Bady to come inside so they can discuss what happened. Bady walks cautiously down the hall where the three men are standing. He tells the sheriff that the investigator from Jackson has arrived.

"Radio back and tell someone to bring him here," instructs the sheriff.

"I already took care of that, he will be here directly."

Bady walks inside the room to witness the carnage for himself. He then steps back outside of the room and shakes his head in disbelief. Bady says, "What we goan do next? This thang keep plucking y'all off one by one."

BillyRay replies, "What do you mean by 'y'all'? You don't have to be related to die. Look what happened to Glenn."

Bady's face turns red as he takes his hat off to scratch his head. He says, "Well, we better hurry up and get that thang befo' someone else dies."

They hear some car doors slam, so they start heading in the direction of whatever or whoever just arrived. The four men meet the investigator as he turns the corner coming from the front of the masion. The investigator has the strangest look on his face as he is greets them. Douglas looks deep into the investigator's eyes and asks,

"What did you find?"

"Some of what I've found, I'm finding it hard to believe myself. We took plaster molds of the prints that were left behind. They were left by a mule or horse. We took samples of flesh off the bodies that were not the flesh of the victims. The flesh had been dead for a long time. The second set of prints we found came from a sheep or goat. The hair samples from all crime scenes were mule and sheep hair. The greenish foul smelling substance could not be identified. We even had it sent to the FBI labs and got the same results. We are dealing with something of the likes that I have never dealt with before."

Douglas replies, "Do you think it was the Haint that did the killin'?"

"When dealing with the unknown, I don't take anything lightly. I grew up being told stories about haints and spirits, by the elders in my family. I have aunts and uncles that have told me they have seen them and have been protected by them. I was always told by the really old folks that haints were good spirits sent here to protect us and that they were the souls of tortured slaves that come back to protect family members from harm. If you hear the chains a rattlin' it be one of dem. If it is a Haint and it is doing all this killing, somebody did something wrong. They say the slave masters made up stories about Haints to keep their slaves from running away at night to escape to freedom. I'll tell you this much, I ain't playing around with whatever is doing the killing. I think we all need to get down on our hands and knees and pray."

The sheriff does not know what to think after hearing Mr. Sunnington's scientific and folklore based evidence. He asks Mr. Sunnington to go study the crime scene inside Thadeus's bedroom. Everyone follows the investigator as he walks toward the back of the house to do his work. Something spooks some chickens and they jump in the sky scaring everyone making their hearts jump out of their chests. All who have guns pulls them out as a result. They all stop in back of the house as he points at three sets of tracks going inside and outside the house. He tells them that the tracks are sheep, mule, and chicken prints. There are feathers and blood at the back door leading into the house. The investigator is studying every aspect of what he thinks might have happened.

The sheriff yells out, "Some dam fool done trained some animals to do the killin' 'round here!" "Now, who the hell would do somethin like that?" replies Bady, "I wish that was the case because we would be looking for someone to arrest. This is not the case. We don't know what we're dealing with. You see, if you look at these bloody prints coming out the bedroom, you can see they are small. If you look at these, they change from the smaller ones of a ram to the larger hooves of a mule."

The four men follow the investigator down the hall as he points out clues and evidence. "I have never seen anything like this before," says Mr. Sunnington, "If there is someone controlling them, it must be a magician in order to make the animal change form."

"How do you know the animal changes form?" replies Bady.

"There are three different kinds of prints here. If there are three animals there would be far more sets of prints randomly everywhere. These prints follow each other in a kinda orderly manner."

The sheriff yells out, while scratching his head, "I don't give a dam! Someone is controlling these dam critters and I don't believe in no nigga spook shit! Now listen, Mr. big shot investigator, stop talkin 'bout that spook shit and just present the evidence. I am ret' to go back to my office and take care of some unfinished business. I will see y'all later." Mr. Sunnington steps in front of the sheriff and begins pointing his fingers in his chest and says, "I'm about nigged out. Um plum tired of that word; y'all wearing it out. I hear it one mo ginn um goan put my foot in somebodies ass. Ya feel me. The sheriff swallows hard because he is shook by Mr. Sunnington and says, "OOOOOh ok, just wound up with dis' killin' 'round here. Just a figure of speech, it wont be said again." Mr Sunnington smiles and says, "Dam show 'preciate it.

He asks Bady for his keys to the police car and tells him to ride back with Douglas and BillyRay. The sheriff waddles back to Bady's car while the four men continue to follow the tracks that leave out the back door going towards the back of the mansion.

The left back side of the mansion is next to the woods which meets the well maintained grass of the new Wellington Estate. Through those woods is where the old mansion stands and even further is the trailer park. When they reach the edge of the woods, where the grass ends and the woods begin, Douglas and BillyRay say at the same time, "I ain't goin' no further. You guys can go if you want to see where the prints end up. But we ain't goin."

Bady replies, "Why y'all gettin' spooked? I already followed the prints coming out of Rose's house in there and nothin' happened to me."

"Well, y'all go on ahead in there, we will be right here waitin' for y'all," replies Douglas..

The Investigator and Bady continue to follow the tracks that are leading to where the old mansion is. Bady taps the investigator on the shoulder and says, "Over yonder is the trailer park. That is the direction I came from before when I followed the prints the last time."

They first pass Granny's old house that lies in ruins. The windows seem to follow the men as if they were eyes on the face of the building. The tracks bring them to a very large oak tree. It is so big and old, it must have been there for at least a few hundred years. The investigator and Bady continue to follow the tracks. He suddenly stops, just as he gets to the other side of the large oak tree. He sees that the prints change form as they come pass the tree. "In fact, it looks like whatever it was, just walked right through the oak tree and changed its form. Whatever it is, did not stay long, it's back out and about," says the investigator.

I don't know about you Bady, but I'm getting the hell out of here," says Yuseph.

The two men draw their pistols and walk sideways, back to back, just to make sure nothing can sneak up from behind. The eyes on Granny's old home follow them the opposite way as they pass again. When they meet Douglas and BillyRay they explain what they just saw and what happened

"Will you guys come back to the house with me so that I can take more samples?"

"All of us?" replies Douglas.

"Yea, I think we all need to stay together. If you notice the only time someone dies is when they are completely by themselves, so I think we should all stay together." Youseph starts walking toward the mansion and the three men look at each other as if to agree with what he said and begin to follow.

The sheriff arrives back at the station. He rolls out of his car and waddles through the front door. He yells out, "EmmaLiz, EmmaLiz!" No one answers. EmmaLiz is the dispatcher for the station. The sheriff begins mumbling and then talking out loud. "Dat dam nigga spook shit got everybody runnin' scared! Blue, Blue, where are you?" The sheriff yells out to Blue, "Are you scared of that spook too?"

Blue is a hound dog that lives at the station. He is white with dark blue spots all over him. He is the station's mascot and the sheriff's personal pet. The sheriff scratches his head and says, "It's too dam quiet 'round here. I don't even hear no chatter on the radio. My dog didn't even run up to me. Something just ain't right."

The sheriff flops down in his big leather chair behind his desk. He begins hearing humming of wade in de wadah. "MMMMMMMMMMM." The sheriff jumps up, grabbing his pistol out of his holster. He says, "Who the hell is that? Show yo' self!"

He waves his gun from side to side ready to shoot anything that moves. He stalks his way through the door, slowly peering out. He does not see anyone or anything so he walks back into his office and sits back in his big, comfortable leather chair. His face gets distorted from the smell of this really bad aroma. He stands up while sniffing at the same time. He yells out, "What the hell is that smell!"

He sits back down and lays his pistol on his desk. He takes his sheriffs' hat off and lays in on the desk. He leans back in his chair and locks his fingers to cradle his head. He is looking around as if he is waiting for something to come. All of a sudden something runs by the door in a blur. It is on all fours and it has a tail. The sheriff jumps as he gets startled by what just happened.

"Blue, Blue, come yo behind chere; I knew you were in here."

The phone rings and the sheriff picks it up. "Hello." He listens as the person speaks and then the sheriff speaks.

"When I got here, it was like a ghost town. EmmaLiz wasn't dispatching on the radio and it was quiet as a church mouse in here."

While the sheriff talks his expression suddenly changes. He says, "Listen Douglas, something smells mighty foul 'round here."

As he talks he notices a tail hanging out the front left hand corner of his desk. He then hears chains rattling. The sheriff says, "Bady and Douglas, y'all head on back to the station so we can discuss everything that has happened thus far. I don't wanna hear no mo.' 'bout that spook shit either. This dog done turned over some garbage and wallowed in it and I got to see at her."

The sheriff slams the phone down in disgust from the smell. As soon as the sheriff hangs the phone up, Douglas realizes that the sheriff was talking about an odor. He immediately redials the sheriff's number to tell him to get out of there. Douglas knows that is the sign of the coming of the Haint. Douglas signals Bady, Youseph, and BillyRay to get in their cars and get to the station. He explains what has just happened while they are on their way to the station. The sheriff stands up saying. "Who done put a chain 'round my Blues neck. They know I don't chain my dog."

The sheriff steps around his desk and starts crouching down as he gets closer to the dog's tail. The phone begins to ring, then suddenly the tail spends around and the sheriff is face to face with Granny, whose head is on the body of a hound dog. The sheriff's facial features get distorted by fear. After she pounces on him, Granny begins ripping and tearing the sheriff's face. The sheriff screams in horror and pain. The screams suddenly become muffled because Granny has him by the throat, with her big sharp teeth, ripping and tearing, as she clamps down. With a sudden jerk of her neck the gurgling stops and the sheriff's body goes limp. The Haint has a freshly ripped throat lodged in her teeth with blood dripping from it. She shakes her head and the lump of flesh dislodges and drops on the floor. As she leaves she wags her tail like a good little doggy.

As he drives, Bady has Douglas on the phone on speaker, explaining to his two partners what happened. Douglas explains, "When the sheriff said he smelled something bad, I knew Granny was near. I tried to tell him to leave but he hung up. He also told me that there was no one in the station which was another sign."

In Chicago, Robert's family is packing for the trip. Marvin's clothes are also packed and he is ready to go to the airport. Marvin's family gathers around him after loading the taxi cab with his luggage. They all look up at him with very worried looks on their faces. He looks down, over and around, surveying them with a strong stern look on his face and recites to them, "Do not worry, I will be just fine." His words somewhat comfort them as they all group hug their father and husband with all their might. He kisses them all on their foreheads before shutting the door to his suburban upper middle class home.

He jumps into a cab that already has been instructed its destination. Marvin's family knows about Granny and does not play with the reality of events that have occurred. Marvin and Robert both arrive at the airport at the same time. They check their bags in and are waiting in line to go to their gate. Robert notices Marvin first and he waves. After being checked in, they sit next to each other at the gate. Marvin waves to the rest of Roberts's family and they smile and wave back.

Marvin says, "Looks like we are going down there for the same thing at the same time."

"Yes, unfortunately that is the case."

"Why aren't you bringing your family?"

"My cousin JeanAnn told me to leave them at home because of what's going on down there." "You really believe in that stuff, don't you?"

"Robert, I do believe in spirits and I don't take anything for granted. Besides, my children have some serious exams coming up and they need to be focused. My cousin RayPaul would understand because he knew how I valued education."

"I value education as well, but my children love their Auntie Rose, so I am bringing them down there."

Robert's phone rings and he answers. "Hello." The features on his face lift as he hears his brother's voice. In an instance his features change from happy to sad from what Douglas has just told him. Robert just found out that his brother Thadeus is dead. He tells his brother he is on his way and slowly hangs up the phone with a dazed look on his face. Marvin asks, "What's wrong?" Robert mumbles something, staring in space in a daze.

"What did you say? I don't understand mumbling."

Robert, with a sad, dazed look on his face says, "My brother Thadeus is dead."

Marvin, shaking his head slowly and speaking softly, whispers to Robert, "I'm sorry to hear that. I guess you will need a few more days other than the ones you already requested."

"I suppose so, Marvin, I suppose so."

Robert puts his head down and tears begin to fall down his cheeks. Robert looks up at Marvin and asks, "How do you stop a Haint?"

"I don't know, but my cousin tells me I need to see the Root Lady. She has been asking for me." "After you talk to her, please contact me so I can know what to do." Marvin hugs his friend and coworker to take some of the hurt off him.

Meanwhile, back in Mississippi, the three men and the young man arrive at the police station. The three officers get into their stalking mode before they get out of their cars. With guns in hand, they walk real lightly, as if they are walking on egg shells They cautiously walk inside the building, guns pointing in every direction.

They first notice the foul smell of rotten eggs and burnt sulfur. Then they see the bloody paw prints coming out the sheriff's office going into Douglas's office. The three men follow the prints with their guns pointed. As they walk into Douglas's office they see the prints go out of his window. They realize that the Haint is gone, so they put their guns back into their holsters.

They all turn around and walk towards the sheriff's office. BillyRay is standing in the hall between the sheriff's office and his uncle's office. When they get to BillyRay he asks, "What happened? What did you see?"

"Nothing," replies Douglas, "whatever happened is done and gone."

The four men walk into the sheriff's office and are horrified at what they see. The face and throat of the sheriff is completely ripped apart. You could not tell it was him if you did not know him yourself. Douglas yells, "EmmaLiz, EmmaLiz! Where is EmmaLiz? Do you think the Haint got her too?"

Bady replies, "I don't know. We are going to have to look 'round here and make sure there ain't another body."

Youseph the investigator yells out, "We gonna need a preacher 'round here!" Bady and Douglas look at Youseph Ali Sunnington like he said something crazy.

"I don't know why y'all looking at me like that, 'cause y'all is the ones she after. So keep not believing in her and see what happens to y'all. Me myself I'm going to gather up the rest of these samples and bring them back to Jackson today. I will get back to y'all as soon as possible." The investigator goes to his car and gets his equipment and begins collecting samples. He wastes no time gathering evidence and putting it away.

BillyRay, Douglas and Bady watch as Mr. Sunnington continues to do his investigative probing not knowing what they are going to do next. Douglas speaks out, "I think we all should stay together until this stuff is over."

Bady replies, "I think you're right, Douglas."

BillyRay yells, "I am tired of that nigga bitch spook! I got something furr her ass!"

He dashes out the door heading for parts unknown. They all run after him but his legs are too fast and too young for them to catch. The two men stop running a few feet after they pass the door. Bady grabs Douglas and says, "All we can do is pray to the Lord to keep him safe."

They both turn toward the door and walk back inside. As they cross the threshold, they hear noises coming from the utility closet. The two men draw their guns and begin stalking towards it. Douglas slowly reaches for the door knob as Bady gets in position to shoot whatever is in there. Douglas then snatches the door open and Bady points at whatever is in there and shouts, "Don't move or I'll shoot! Put your hands in the air where I can see dem."

They slowly see two hands rise from behind a broken desk, followed by arms. They hear a voice, "Please don't shoot me."

The person is in plain view and quickly jumps out from behind an old desk, shouting, "Bady, Douglas!" She then runs to them with open arms. They both say at the same time, "You were in there this whole time."

She looks at them both with fear in her eyes and asks, "Is she still here?"

Douglas replies, "Is who still here?"

"I seen her, I seen her!"

"You seen who?"

"I seen the Haint! I heard the humming of 'Wade in the water' and I looked around to see who was doing it cuz' it sounded really nice. As I turned around I was face to face with her, she told me to leave cuz' she ain't got no dealin's with me. She had really sharp teeth, green stuff coming out the middle of her head and she smelled really bad. Her head was on the body of Blue. I heard the sheriff come in, but I did not want to say anything because I was scared. Is he all right?" Both men put their heads down. Douglas looks up and says, "No Emma, he's dead. The Haint got him too."

"What do you mean got him too?" interrupts EmmaLiz. "I know all 'bout the killin's and the curse. I am related to the black Wellingtons and I been told this story since I was knee high to a curb. We have a Haint that watches over us on my father's side but it don't do no killin'."

Douglas replies, "Its killin' people that ain't even related to us, why is that?" "I recon' if ya cursin' it and don't believe in it, that makes you fair game. Haints only come out when the moon is full. She kills when she gets ready. She done got some bad roots or somethin'. I ain't saying no mo.' I don't want her to be after me." Douglas asks, "What do we do to stop her?" "Y'all better get down on yo hands and knees and pray," says Mr. Sunnington.

Douglas quickly goes in his office and does just that. He gets down on his hands and knees and starts praying. Bady stands in the doorway watching and shaking his head. Douglas looks up and says, "Why are you looking at me like that? You better do the same 'cause you are in this too." She killed Glenn and the sheriff and neither one of them is related to us. I know now not to disrespect Granny Haint. We just need to find out what she wants so she can stop doin' all of this killin'."

"I ain't seen it, so I don't believe it," says Bady, "for all I know, it be some crazy ass fool doin' all this." In the back of his mind he knows what he has already seen and he is trying to dismiss it and not believe.

"What more info do you need?" replies Douglas. "The report Mr. Sunnington gave us and everything else that is going on ain't proof enough?"

"I'll believe it when I see it."

"You better hope it's not too late, cuz' you may meet her. If you think about it, the people that have been dying are the ones that really cursed her badly."

"I ain't talkin bout her, I just ain't seen her," says Bady

Bady stands there zoning, looking into space when he feels something tickling his hand. He feels wetness on his fingers. He snatches his hand away stepping back at the same time. With his gun drawn he looks down where the sensation he was feeling on his hand was coming from. It is Blue the hound dog who cowers from the action of Bady. Bady calls him with kindness which changes Blues demeanor. Blue walks over to him and Bady begins to pet him saying. "Where the hell you been? Why aint you gone after that Haint ?" Blue looks back up at him whining as if to say "What the hell you want me to do? That's your job. I ain't fuckin with her." Douglas pauses for a moment as he thinks who has bad mouthed her the most. He yells out, "BillyRay!"

Douglas turns, grabs his hat and starts running to his car. He tells Bady, "Come on we don't have much sun light left, it will be dark in a short short." Before leaving, Bady tells EmmaLiz to stay by the radio in case someone calls about BillyRay. EmmaLiz answers back, "I will stay because I don't think she's coming back. At least, I hope not." Bady and Douglas ride together for comfort and protection. They are going places they think BillyRay would go. They are canvassing everything with their eyes hoping to catch a glimpse of him.

BillyRay is on his way back to the trailer park. He decides to cut through a patch of woods that is a shortcut to his home. As he walks he begins to hear that all familiar humming. He quickly grabs a tree limb off the ground to protect himself. He yells out, "I ain't scared of you. You come on out so's I can bust yo head wide open." His face frowns from the very bad smell that surrounds him.

He hears a voice and chains rattling. "You done mouthed me the most so's umm goan kill you, boy." BillyRay spins around and around to make sure he is not attacked from behind. He yells out again, "Come on out, you nigga bitch, I got something furr ya!" BillyRay hears the crackling of leaves, so he turns around to confront her, but nothing is there. All of a sudden, he is driven to the ground and saliva and fangs are in his face. Granny is still in the form of Blue. She reaches down with her mouth to BillyRay's mouth and rips out his tongue, jumps off him and disappears. BillyRay staggers to get to his feet. Parts of both lips are missing and a few teeth, and of course the tongue has been ripped clean out of his mouth. He gets to his feet staggering, blood flowing out his mouth like the River Jordon. In a state of shock he still tries to bad mouth Granny but nothing comes out but gurgling of blood. He hears Granny again, "What boy, Granny got your tongue? Haaa, Haaa, Hee, Hee!"

BillyRay is turning around, trying to see where Granny is. He sees the tree limb and picks it up, blood still pouring out all over his body. Bady and Douglas are still riding around looking for BillyRay. They decide to head toward the trailer park because they are not far from there. They both think he is on his way back home. Granny continues to torment BillyRay. She pounces on him and pushes him to the ground. She move so fast she appears as a blur. BillyRay swings at pure air. He is bloody and staggering. He can barely lift the tree limb. He stands there, hunched over, barely able to hold it up. All of a sudden he hears, "You hoo!" He turns around lifting the tree limb to give her his last shot. Granny has turned back into a mule bodied Haint. She has her hind quarters turned his way with her hind legs raring to kick. Her head is turned facing him so she can see what she is doing. Before she flings her hind legs that are her lethals, she says, "I got chow, bitch!" and kicks BillyRays head clean off his body. His lifeless, headless body falls to the ground

BillyRay's head is launched into the air like a football during kick off. Douglas and Bady happen to be coming down the side road leading to the trailer park. They suddenly hear a thud. Something hit their police car and bounced off landing on the side of the road. Douglas slams on the breaks to see what hit them. They both get out of the car with guns drawn. Douglas looks down and he is horrified at what he see's. He yells out, "NOOOOOOOO!"

Douglas starts crying as he talks to the disfigured head saying, "We told you not to leave!"

Bady says, "We goan have to call for back up to find the body. Judging from where it hit us, it musta come from that patch of woods ova' yonda'."

Douglas points his gun into the woods that join the trailer park which is a part of the Wellington estate. Douglas' eyes are full of tears as he walks back to his car holding his nephew's head. Bady hands him a dark plastic trash bag that he has taken from the back seat and asks Douglas for the keys. He tells Douglas, "You ain't in any condition to do any drivin'. Come on, let's head back to the office."

Chapter XXIII

Marvin and Robert are seated in isle seats next to each other. Robert's phone rings and he looks around making sure no stewardess sees him answering it. He shakes his head and puts the phone back into his pocket. Marvin asks him, "Why didn't you answer your phone?"

"I saw that the number was from home, so I didn't answer. I don't want to hear any more bad news."

"I know what you mean." replies Marvin.

"Yea Marvin, when you go see the Root Lady I want to go, ok"

"I ain't playing around with that Haint. If she wants me to leave, I will leave. I think there has been too much disrespect shown to her. There has been too much killing going on and it has to stop." says Marvin.

Robert looks at Marvin with a funny look. He says, "I knew you were some kin' to me. I knew it all along."

"How did you know that, and where did you get your info from?"

"The first time I went into your house I saw pictures of home. That gave me an idea. Your name Wellington was a giveaway."

"Yea, yea, yea, Robert; I knew you were my cousin also. I just didn't say anything either. That's why I been going out my way to help you and keep you close," replies Marvin with a comforting smile on his face. "Robert, let's go down there and ask grand ma' to stop killing our family."

Back at the police department in BrookHaven, Bady and Douglas are carrying BillyRays head into the building. As they walk through the door EmmaLiz says, "What do you guys got in the bag?"

"EmmaLiz, you really don't want to know."

They stop and tell her what happened. Douglas walks into the kitchen and he puts his nephews head in the freezer. After he shuts the freezer's door, he leans on the refrigerator and begins to cry. Bady walks over to Douglas and puts his arm around him patting him on the shoulder. Douglas raises his head off the arm that he was crying on and says, "Bady, I need a good night sleep, I am so so tired."

"Douglas, I agree witcha. I need some sleep really bad too. I been up as long as you have."

Bady and Douglas start walking out the door, EmmaLiz wave as they pass her. They both jump into their cars and roll out in opposite directions.

Bady arrives at his house first because he lives closer to work than Douglas. He sluggishly gets out of his car and tries to open his front door fumbling his keys while doing so. After successfully opening his door he immediately pulls his gun out and walks in. Upon entry he has a very eerie feeling. He smells the foul smell that was present at the other murders. He yells out, "I ain't scared of you. You come out so's I can see ya!" He goes from room to room pointing his gun, ready to let off shots at whatever he discovers that doesn't belong in his home. The last room to be checked is the kitchen. He cautiously walks into the kitchen and there is no one there. The garbage is over flowing and smells really bad.

He puts his gun on the counter and grabs another trash bag out of the cabinet. He pushes the trash down into the trash bag, pulls it out of the can, ties it up to bring it outside.

"That was the foul smell I had smelled."

He throws it over his back and opens the back door. He walks over to the trash can, takes off the lid and drops the trash into the garbage can. As soon as he turns around he is face to face with Granny. They are looking straight into each other's eyes. The green stuff is oooozing out of her forehead, and saliva is dripping down her fangs.

"I'ze got no dealing with you, all I want to know is, do you believe?"

Bady can't believe what he is seeing. He starts muttering, "I,I,I,I,I,I,I," Granny replies, "That ain't quick enough."

She immediately begins ripping and tearing him apart. Her head is on the body of a mule; ripping and tearing his face; then she transforms her head to the body of a rooster. Then she rams him into the wall as a sheep and cocks her leg and pisses on him after transforming herself into a dog. She then changes to a black cat while daintily walking around swaying her tail observing her carnage. As she walks away from Badys' lifeless body, she starts going through all of her different metamorphoses, cat to mule to ram to rooster then a dog, as if to show off her diabolical superiority. Bady's lifeless mutilated body is slumped over next to the trash can that is against the wall of his house.

Roberts wife informs Marvin and Robert that there will be a delay in their transfer flight to Jackson. The next flight will not be leaving until the morning. They both shake their heads and slump in their seats. The morning comes and Marvin and Robert arrive at the Jackson airport. They get off the plane and head over to the baggage claim department. Marvin says, "Robert, I am going to rent a car, you can ride with me if you want to." Everyone wipes the sweat off thier foreheads, created by the mid morning Mississippi heat

"Thanks Marvin. That will be fine because I did not notify anyone about the exact time of my arrival. When I get home I will be able to use a number of cars to get around in." Marvin's phone rings and he picks it up. He listens as the person is speaking to him. "Listen JeanAnn, you stay right there, I will be there as soon as possible." Marvin shakes his head as he hangs up his cell phone.

"Robert, you guys can stand outside with me while we wait for the shuttle to bring us to the rent a car place."

They waddle through the glass sliding doors with their luggage in tow. They place their luggage on the curb and wait for the shuttle. While waiting, Robert asks Marvin to bring him to Douglas's house so he can get the keys to Thadeus's house because that is where they will be staying. When they arrive at the rent a car agency, Marvin rents a burgundy Lincoln Navigator. They load it up and roll out.

Meanwhile, back in Brookhaven, Douglas is still in his bed sleeping. It is almost noon and he has gotten sleep that he really needs. He is tossing and turning in his sleep. He is mumbling things that only he can understand. He frantically jumps up, face covered in sweat, pajamas twisted and wrinkled, and begins looking around the room. The AC in his room is blowing cold air. The sweat on his face begins to dry. He leans over and grabs his cell phone off the night stand and begins dialing. He is waiting and anticipating for someone to pick up. No one answers. He hangs up and dials again to no avail. Whoever he is calling is not home or just not picking up the phone. Douglas slams the lid of his cell phone down. He is sitting up in his bed, legs crossed like a Native American. He brings his legs up in a fetal position, rests his arms on his knee caps and begins to cry.

Douglas had a dream that Granny was attacking Bady. That is why he woke up in a bad way. Since he did not get an answer to his phone call, he assumes the worst. He just wants to jump up and go over there. Being drunk with sorrow from all the murders, all he wants is to wait for his emotions to sober up. He calls EmmaLiz at the station to have a couple of cars go over Bady's and investigate. After he hangs up with EmmaLiz he slumps back into a horizontal fetal position. He stares at the wall with a blank look on his face.

"What do you suppose will happen when we get home?" asks Robert.

"I really don't know. JeanAnn was on her way to pick me up, I told her to go back because I was renting a car."

JeanAnn and Marvin are very close. They spent a lot of time around each other every time Marvin came to Mississippi for the summer. She is related to Marvin by marriage.

"JeanAnn wants me to see the Root Lady really bad. I don't know why, but the Root Lady wants to see me as well."

"Maybe you have something to do with stopping her" replies Robert.

"You mean you really believe in her, Marvin?"

"I would have to say, yes I do. How many times do I have to tell you man? She has been part of our family's history too long for me not to. I even tell my daughters sometimes, 'Y'all better be good, or Granny's goan get y'all. I saw her when I was a little chap, we use to come down here every summer to visit our kin' folks. They would always tell us about her, especially when we were bad. One hot summer night my uncle was telling the story to a whole bunch of us sitting on his porch. I was not paying attention because I did not believe in it. I was wiggling stuff in people's ears and making strange noises to distract them. I was thirteen at the time and I thought I was grown. My uncle stopped talking and looked in my direction with the meanest look you could imagine and said, 'Boy, if you don't wanna listen, carry yo narrow ass way from 'round here.'

I jumped off the porch and started walking down the dirt road to my other uncle's house. My cousins shouted 'Guanna goan get ya, Guanna goan get ya!' I looked back and the rest of my cousins were looking at my uncle as if they could see the words coming out his mouth. You know where we live it's a little village and we all stayed not far from each other. As I was walking, I smelt a very bad smell and I wondered where it was coming from. I thought it was something that died. I heard chains rattling then I began hearing the humming of one of those old church hymns, 'Wade in the water, wade in the water children.' I thought it was one of my aunts coming to get me for acting up. The humming was coming from my uncle's old house where he lived before he moved in with his daughter. I crept around the side of the house to scare whoever was doing the humming. I jumped out from the side of the house and said boo! It was a mule with its tail swishing off the late night summer heat. I could not move because I was too scared. The head slowly turned around. The mule's body had an old woman's head on it. She winked her eye and said, "Do you believe in me now?" "I slowly nodded my head yes." she said, "Well, good, now goan."

I turned around and took off. I was running so fast I did not feel my feet hitting the ground. I ran past my uncles and the rest of my cousins sitting on the porch. I opened the door and ran into one of the bedrooms, jumped in the bed and pulled the sheet over my head. I heard shuffling coming towards me. I knew it was my uncle cuz' that was the way he walked. He had a grin on his face as if he knew what had happened. 'I done told ya boy, don't play with Granny.' He turned around and started shuffling out the bed room laughing as hard as he could.

I will never forget that as long as I live. The part of land my aunts and uncles live on and worked has been in our family since we were freed from slavery. The land was once a part of the Wellington plantation. It has been in our family since after the Civil War.

Every July 13 our family has a big cook out. We eat, drink and go visit a part of our land where I think the massacre took place. We would all gather 'round a small fenced in the area where flowers are neatly kept and a large wooden cross is in the middle of. The preacher man would say a prayer then we would all sing 'Wade in the water' as we walk away from the site. The pace would be slow and low as we sang. The further we got away the louder and funkier we would sing, until we were dancing and shouting the words out of our mouths. We did this year after year, ever since I could remember. I think that is where the mass killing took place. No one really ever spoke out much about what happened but they would always mention being good befo Granny get ya."

Robert looks at Marvin as if he could see what he is saying. "If you had not been so bad that night you would have heard the whole story," says Robert while looking at Marvin with a 'matter of fact' look on his face. Then he asks, "Marvin, what are we going to do about this?" Marvin has a very unsure look on his face and says, "I don't right know."

When they arrive at Douglas's house Robert hops out of the truck and rings Douglas's door bell. Douglas jumps up after hearing the sound of the doorbell. He quickly gets out of bed and puts his pants on, zipping them as he hobbles down the stairs. Douglas opens the door and embraces his brother Robert. Robert waves for Marvin to come to the front door where he and Douglas are waiting. When Marvin gets to the door Robert asks if they knew one another. They both say at the same time, "Oh yea Robert, I know him."

Douglas says, "You some kin' to RayPaul and dem. I've seen you in and around these parts for years."

Douglas shepherd's them into the house with his long out reaching arm. They go into the living room and sit on the sofa. Douglas begins telling them everything in detail that has happened thus far. The two men sit there with shock and fear written all over their faces.

Marvin says, "Well, I got to go see the Root Lady. JeanAnn tells me she wants to see me really bad."

"Good luck," replies Douglas. "We went there and we did not get a lick of information."

Robert replies, "Marvin, I want to go with you."

"I don't know, I think I need to go by myself."

Douglas tells Robert to take his luggage off the truck, that he would take them over Thadeus's himself.

Marvin replies, "I want to take you there myself so I can know where Thadeus lives in case you need to be picked up. Douglas says, "That sounds like a plan." He turns around and faces the entrance. He stretches his long arms and puts his hands together as if he was praying, yawning at the same time. They shake Douglas's hand and walk out the door, going towards the truck, when Marvin says, "I know where your brother lives. I said I would bring you because Douglas needs some sleep. He probably has been up ever since this stuff started happening. If he took y'all over Thadeus's house, he probably would have continued to stay up. Let that man rest. I need to hurry and drop y'all off cuz' I want to see the Root Lady before it gets dark. There are things I need to know today."

Robert's wife and children don't seem to be bothered at all. They seem to be very calm and collected. Robert, on the other hand, looks grief stricken and unsure of himself.

"Isn't his house on the other side of the trailer park, right before you get to Springfield?"

"Yea man, that's where he lives."

They pull up to the mourning mansion that has lost its lord and master. Robert Wellington and his family start taking their luggage out of the truck bringing it into the mansion with the help of Marvin. When everything is loaded into the house, Marvin and Robert embrace before Marvin goes on his mission to the Root Lady's house. Marvin says, "Make sure you call me if something strange happens."

"I will," replies Robert. As Marvin leaves, Robert signals for him to roll his window down.

"Marvin, call me as soon as you get any information from the Root Lady."

Marvin nods his head yes as he heads north toward the Root Lady's house.

Marvin starts driving towards the Root Lady's house when it hits him and he realizes that he needs to see JeanAnn and get the exact directions because he is not sure exactly where she lives.

When he reaches JeanAnn house she is sitting on the porch as if she is waiting for him. When he steps up on the porch they hug each other tightly. She says, "Now Marvin RayPaul is gone and I don't want to talk about her at all. You can stay here cuz' we got a plenty of space. I would unpack and relax before going to see the Root Lady."

"I will do just that JeanAnn, I just don't want to go there too late." The sun is starting to drop and Marvin decides it is time to make his journey. He hugs JeanAnn and they touch knuckles before he leaves.

He really doesn't know what to expect. He begins to hum Granny's hymn to himself. He pulls over and parks on the side of the road next to the path leading to the Root Lady's house. There are only a couple hours of day light left, so he wants to get to her house as soon as possible. He begins walking up the path leading to her shack. The bushes seem to lean away from the path, as if they were saluting and inviting Marvin to the front door. As he reaches up to knock, the door slowly opens by itself. Marvin pokes his head inside the door and says, "Hello, hello, is anyone home?"

He hears a voice speak out that startles him.

"Come on in son."

He creeps in the room, looking around to see where the voice is coming from. His head and eyes stop roaming as they are fixed on a short purpled haired elderly African American woman. She calls him closer, using her long inward curling finger nails. He hesitantly eases closer. She looks at him and says,

"You da only one dat can stop her. See, you done saw her and you believe in her. You are smart and the most like her than all yo kin'. I done told ya all um goan say, na get 'cause she may come see me fo' tellin' you dis."

"Will you be ok?"

"Like my great grands say, 'Um from the dirty dirty, what it do."

Marvin smiles at the old woman as she ushers him out the door. He hears some creeks as the door closes itself back. He pulls out his cell phone and calls Robert. Marvin says, "Robert, I have some good news to tell you. I am on my way back to your brother's house to share what the Root Lady told me."

While Marvin was talking to Robert, Robert picks up a picture of him Douglas, Rose, Mary and Thadeus. He stares at it in a daze. Marvin is getting no response from Robert. Marvin says, "Robert, are you there, are you there?"

Robert snaps out of his daze and says, "Yea, yea man, come on over. I'm ready for some good news."

They both hang up their phones at the same time. Marvin continues to drive and Robert slowly places the picture on the table. Robert has two boys and two girls. The girls are ages nine and twelve. The boys are fourteen and sixteen. They are all unpacking except for the two girls. Their mother is unpacking for them. The two girls ease out the front door to go out and play. Lisa is the older of the two and she leads the way. They both hear this sweet humming coming from the woods. It puts them in a trance like state as they follow the sweet sound into the woods toward the old mansion. There is an unusual breeze blowing through the two girls long blond hair.

The boys run up to their father and ask him if he knows where the girls have gone. They also alert their mother and they all begin to search the house. They all meet up at the front door and no one seems to know the girls' location. The youngest boy opens the door and goes running out toward the woods. Marvin pulls up and hurries out of the truck after seeing Robert's family in such a frantic state. Marvin says,

"What's going on, what's happening?"

"We don't know where the girls are, and Joseph Anthony went running into the woods looking for them."

The two men take off into the woods with Roberts's wife and Robert Jr. following. When they reach the oak tree near the old mansion they all stop in their tracks. The oak tree is tall and has a very wide trunk. As it rises up, part of the trunk seems to bend with a bulge on one side, as if someone was frozen in place trying to shake their booty. At the top of the tree there are very long vines that reach out and are gripping all the front windows of the old mansion. They seem to be pulling at the frame work because the front of the old mansion is leaning toward the tree. Granny has Jo Anthony and the two girls standing in front of her in a trance like state, waiting for the two men to arrive. Even though its evening this event makes the night come faster and it begins to get darker.

Granny speaks out. "Y'all gonna witness the massacre of yo' family just like I witnessed the massacre of mine fo generations back."

Marvin speaks out. "You shouldn't do that Granny. You are the matriarch of our family and theirs. Our daughters look up to you for wisdom and guidance. You are their role model for being a strong, black woman."

As Marvin is saying this, Granny's features begin to soften. The mule bodied woman seems to be adjusting to his kind words.

"Well, I been part of this old oak tree for a many moons. I've seen my people come and go. Y'all kept me alive by believing in me and telling stories."

She looks at Robert saying, "I remember y'all playing around here when y'all was iddy biddy chaps. That was me giving y'all that cold feeling. I was not going to get none of my peoples, but RayPaul was going to warn Thadeus' great, great, great, great grands, so I had to kill him. He was just like his great, great, great, great grandfather; ol' dumb ass nigga."

Robert comes up with enough courage to speak and says, "We are good people. You suppose to get the bad and evil people."

Marvin looks at Robert as if he has said too much. Marvin cries out, "Granny, we's pleadin with ya, you're free Granny, you're free!"

Out of nowhere, Youseph Ali Sunnington and Douglas walk up and stand next to Robert and Marvin. Mr. Sunnington stands next to Robert and Douglas stands next to Marvin, keeping Marvin and Robert in the middle. They are almost in a trance like state as they watch Granny. Granny's face and pupils begin to have color. Her eyes even twinkle from what Marvin has just said to her. The fangs in her mouth draw back into her gums and the hole in her forehead disappears. Her raspy coarse voice begins to soften as she speaks. This transformation happens as the sun is setting. The body of the mule becomes the body of a beautiful old corn rolled haired African American woman. While this transformation is happening the boy and the two girls run over to their mother who is standing a few feet behind the men.

Granny looks up into the sky with both hands raised while saying something in her native tongue. She slowly walks over to Robert and Marvin. Douglas and Mr. Sunnington step back as if they have been a part of this ritual before. She takes both hands and rubs the faces of Robert and Marvin with one stroke, making their faces into one. She looks in their faces and says with a very clear voice, "I am free, my children, I am free; at last I am free."

The two girls slowly walk up to Granny as if they are walking in a wedding, so they can touch her long flowing gown. She touches their foreheads as if she is anointing them. "Y'all are of my essence and I will watch ova y'all OK. The two girls nod their heads yes and walk back to their mother. As the sun is setting, it is getting darker as Granny turns toward the end of the plantation where the massacre took place. A bright light begins to emanate from there. It begins to overpower the place of the setting sun, which is dropping over the horizon. It is all Granny's children and grandchildren are coming towards her in a big ball of light. She holds out her arms as they touch and hug her on their way to the tree. Everyone stands in awe of what they are seeing. One by one, they disappear into the tree after paying Granny her respect, thanking her for freeing them. She smiles at everyone as she backs into the tree. She begins to immerse herself into the deep split in the center of the tree.

Before she completes her metamorphosis, she calls Marvin to her and whispers, "To the east of this here tree dig three and always remember, it is more in takin' care of then makin'. Marvin smiles as he backs up. Just as she is almost completely dissolved in the tree she quickly pops her head out of the split in the tree, with fangs drawn, colorless pupils, and green ooze coming out the center of her forehead, looking into Roberts eyes, with a coarse and raspy voice she says, "Na Robert, remember what you said."

Then her head disappears back into the tree. A large beam of light shoots out of the top of the tree and when it reaches the sky there is an explosion of light like fireworks shooting sparkles. Each face of those who were killed by Thadeus, as well as Granny's face, can clearly be seen before shooting into the universe.

Marvin gets a good idea of what Granny meant as he looks at Robert with disappointment. Robert looks over at Marvin shrugging his shoulders saying,

"What did I say? What did I say? I didn't mean no harm."

They all walk in the direction of Thadeus's house not knowing what will happen next.

Chapter XXIV

Days go by and family members attend funerals. Everything is almost back to normal. Douglas is the sheriff of the town and he resides in Thadeus's house. Marvin digs down three feet at the east of the tree and unearths an old wooden churn. It is heavy as he struggles to pull it out the hole. He pry's the top off and gold silver coins of all types spill over the top of the churn. In his mind he envisions, Granny's house being restored and a large mansion with many rooms next to it. This house will be for family and they will always have somewhere to stay when they come to visit.

Marvin and Robert meet each other at Thadeus's house. Robert and his family are packing a minivan when Marvin pulls up. Marvin gets out of a car that he borrowed from JeanAnn and walks over to Robert saying, "Listen man, I am taking this truck back to JeanAnne and hopping on the next thang smokin to go back home. I have had enough of this country town for now. I'm going home. Take your time driving back, I got you covered." Robert looks into Marvin's eyes as they embrace, and he thanks him.

Marvin hops back into his car and takes off. Robert puts the last bag in the hatch of his minivan and tries to shut it. Robert's wife gets out of the minivan to see what the problem is and begins to help Robert shut the hatch. Robert asks his wife, "We did not bring that much stuff. Why is it so hard to shut this hatch? What did you put in there?"

"Nothing honey," she replies as their combined effort shuts the hatch. They both get back in the van and pull off.

As they pull off a beautiful rainbow appears in the sky and the muffled sound of that old familiar Negro spiritual begins to permeate from the loaded back of the van, as they head back to Chi town.

""Wade in de wadah, wade in de wadah, cheeren."

The End

● ● ●

The Haint is an African European and American Folklore and culture meshed together to create an exciting mysterious and tantalizing novel. It has Voodoo, murder, rape, sex, exploitation, healing, loyalty, love, universal oneness and living biblical comparisons. *The Haint* is also about the duality between the good and evil that we all inately have inside us. It starts in Africa and travels across the Atlantic to precivil war America. Come and take the journey.

 *I wrote this book, after hearing my parents talk about Haints through out my life. In fact my father said he shot at one while on guard duty in Japan during World War Two. I went to school in Springfield Ma. I have a Bachelors in Rehab. Counseling and Masters*

In Education to be a Vice Principal. I was always interested in history and all cultures, especially black cultures. As a child my imagination was vivid. I wanted to be an Egyptian Pharaoh to a Viking King.

The power is in the masses, we make history because we are history. Live love dream and read on. I hope this book stimulates your mind as well as the ones that will come after. Us is We, Peace and Love All.

Made in the USA
Middletown, DE
10 September 2015